Blood in the Water

A Combat Memoir of a U.S. Air Force
Marine in the Vietnam War

Larry Stoddard!

Notice

This book is a memoir of events that happened in the author's life. While the author has made every attempt to portray the events as accurately as possible, the confusion of combat mixed with the fog of time may render some scenes differently than others may recall.

Printed in the United States of America

Cover Layout by Morwenna Rakestraw

Version 1.3

ISBN 978-1-940554-24-2
eBook ISBN-978-1-940554-25-9

First Edition December 2014

To Bill Martin

Introduction

In May 2012, I was in the market for a new vehicle. My thirteen year old pickup was starting to give me trouble, and with this "throw away" world we live in, I was being told, "Gee, a truck that old, you can't even get parts for it anymore."

So here I was, in a new dealership. It is well respected and one of the largest new pick-up truck dealers in the Massachusetts-Connecticut area. On one wall, they had a large board that was signed with all kinds of signatures, most of them showing their military rank and where they served. I inquired about the board and my salesman said that they were giving discounts of one thousand dollars off to veterans.

"Oh," I said. "I'm a veteran."

The salesman stopped and looked at me like I was kidding. He saw an elderly grey haired man sitting across from him and just continued like he didn't hear me.

I continued, "Look I'll bring in my DD 214 discharge papers if you want."

You see that one thousand dollars off looked really good to me.

He said, "What war?"

"Vietnam," I replied.

He said something like, "Wrong war," or something like that. I really couldn't pick it up.

I started to get a little insulted. If this truck I wanted was available anywhere else, I would have walked out, but I wanted a standard shift pick-up, full size, and you just can't buy standard shifts anymore. This one was the only one I could find in six states.

Well anyway, I was getting a little put out by his attitude, and I started to insist. The salesman was getting a little put out and said, "Look, I'll go speak to my boss."

So I waited.

About five minutes later he came back and said, "Look we will credit you one hundred dollars, and that is the best we can do."

I said, "Okay," but was thinking, *Why don't I qualify like the new vets?*

I know I wasn't in a popular war, and when we were discharged, we were told we should take our uniforms off as soon as we can.

* * *

Now, I'm for giving the veterans their just recognition and support they earned. So I bought my truck, and after all the hassle, I never did get my one hundred dollar credit. The more I thought about it the more upset I became. The more upset I became the more determined I became to write about my small contribution to the Vietnam war effort, take it back to the dealer and stuff it right up his ass.

So with that in mind, I have taken keyboard in hand and compiled what my war was like in Vietnam. I know, and want it to be known, that I had it very good in The Nam. I served with the Third Marines for a short time, then left for the soft life on a secure base. I did what I was told to do. The guys in the bush and humping the mountains, plains, and jungles were the heroes. I couldn't even believe that anyone could dare say to anyone of them that, "You're really not a vet. You were in the wrong war."

Go tell that to the fifty five thousand names on the wall. If they could speak I bet they would beg to differ. So here is my story. Not for me, but for them. Remember, it has been said, "All gave some, some gave all."

Chapter 1

God, how time flies.

It seems only yesterday I was a young man. Now, as I get closer to the three quarters of a century mark, you really realize that you sure don't have as far to go as you have come. When a person gets along in years and they look forward, there isn't much to look at, not much at all. About the only thing that brings a smile to your face are memories, and I sure am blessed with a full life of memories.

My father, the great man that he was, never had much money, but he had a heart of gold and the willpower to work at two jobs: one fulltime at a shop from 3 p.m. to 11 p.m. and one 7 a.m. to 12 noon as a mechanic at a local garage. I never heard him complain once. He and my mom, who worked at different local stores, raised four kids and did an outstanding job of it.

As for myself, I've never married or had children, but I have heard that when a child is born, they do not come with an instruction booklet. In the old days, before the government started telling parents how to raise their kids, parents seem to have done a lot better job at it. Of course, what has the government ever taken over that it hasn't made worse? But, there has been volumes written on that subject and they never learn.

I wasn't a very bright child, but I was gifted with good health and average memory. One of the things I remember my father and other older people I knew seemed to agree on was that as you get older, "it is always better to wear out rather than rust out." I thought that was a neat saying and it has stuck with me.

Something else that has stuck with me is war. I'm not the only one I'm sure.

I didn't mention earlier that one other thing I was blessed with was luck. Some people have more than their share and I am one of those people. I can even say, I was lucky to graduate high school. I already stated I wasn't that bright. But, I did graduate and with that diploma, I was out in the big world. I was smart enough to know that college was out for me and so was my uncle. Everyone knew him, Uncle Sam. You see, when I graduated from high school, there was a war on and this country had a thing called the Draft. That meant that if you were of the age of 18 and not married with dependents or enrolled in college, you could be drafted into the United States Army for a period of two years. All that was required was that you pass the Army physical: no ifs, ands, or buts. So that meant I was a prime candidate to be drafted. If you didn't want to be drafted, you were free to join any of the other branches of the services.

Well, I figured I'd work that first summer after I graduated from High School and see what developed. The following September, I got my notice from Uncle Sam to report to Boston for my physical prior to being drafted. I had pretty well made up my mind that I didn't want the Army. so before the date of the physical, I went and enlisted into the U.S. Air Force. The catch was, when you enlisted, you had to go for four years, not two. Okay, I liked the uniforms. So why not the Air Force?

So like millions before me, I bid farewell to my family and friends and on 14 Sept 1965, I was sworn into the service of the U.S. Government Department of Air Force. I was scheduled to take my basic training at Lackland Air Force Base San Antonio, Texas, and so for the first time in my life,

I flew in a jet airplane. It first landed in the State of Georgia, where I couldn't understand what people said. From there, to basic training in Texas. In Texas, I learned that there are people out there in the world that aren't very nice. I kept my mouth shut and graduated 8 weeks later. I was told I would be working in supply (not a bad job, I heard). I went home on a ten day leave and while at home, I got orders to report to Whiteman Air Force Base outside Kansas City, Missouri.

Chapter 2

1965-66

I reported to Whiteman AFB in November of 1965. The base wasn't a typical Air Force Base, as the saying goes. First, there were no planes, just helicopters. This was because it was a ballistic missile base that supported Minuteman missiles sited all over the state. The base was a glider training base during World War II. The whole area around the base was flat, and one could understand why it would be ideal for glider training.

Gliders were an important part of the allied invasion of France and D-Day during the war. After the war, the base was just about forgotten until the Cold War with Russia started. For a while, it was a long range jet bomber base and was home to a then top-of-the-line jet bomber called the B-47. Those bombers didn't last too long and were soon phased out as the new and improved bomber, called the B-52, was introduced. The B-52 never made it to Whiteman as far as I knew, but with the new bomber, came the introduction of the long-range ballistic missile of the time.

The Minuteman missile was a state of the art, long-range missile that was fired out of an underground silo where it was kept at the ready at all times. A crew was on duty twenty-four-seven at the missile site. They lived in a bomb proof bunker with the missile, and there was only one doorway to the underground unit. The crew was changed every couple of days.

Being underground as they were, the silos could be placed anywhere (in a field, behind a housing neighborhood) and the average person wouldn't even know. All the crew changes and maintenance were brought in by chopper, so there was very little intrusion to the surrounding area.

The missiles themselves had a range of thousands of miles and were considered the perfect weapon to deter the Russians or anyone else who might be thinking of attacking the United States. They were considered one of the most important weapons we had in those days. Whiteman was only there to support the missiles and served as a supply point for the Boeing Company that had invented the missile and was in charge of keeping the missiles ready and up to date. The Boeing Company had a huge population of workers on-base. They were all civilian, but did all the important maintenance on the missiles.

So after flying to Kansas City, Missouri and taking a bus to a place called Knob Noster, Missouri, about 60 miles east of Kansas City, I reported into the base. Now, due to the fact I had gone home on leave instead of reporting directly to the base after basic training, I reported late and all supply positions were filled. So therefore, I became what is known as "Spare Parts." I didn't learn until later in life that being listed as "Spare Parts" had its advantages.

As I said, when I arrived on-base and reported in, all the supply jobs that were vacant on-base had been filled. There were no requirements for bodies in the base supply system; no fork truck drivers, no warehouse men, no delivery men needed. so what to do with this new boot? Well upon check-in, the powers that be noticed that an obscure position requiring a supply officer was to be posted to another unit on the flight line. The position was now run by a Sergeant, but someone noticed he had put in for a transfer to another base. If he got transferred, the position would be vacant. So Airman Third Class Stoddard AF#

11468827 was assigned to Consolidated Line Maintenance as the Supply Officer, pro tem.

Line Maintenance was in charge of all flight line aircraft, a couple of small twin engine planes, and about 15 Huey helicopters. It sounded pretty good to me. Furthermore, this position was in charge of supplying anything required of the large civilian group assigned by the Boeing Company to keep the numerous Minuteman missiles operational.

The Sergeant currently filling my position had been on-base about 3 years and was a great guy. His name was Whitaker. I forget his first name, but everyone just called him "Whit," anyway. He was a career man and wanted to expand his knowledge of the service, so had requested a transfer. Whit showed me the ropes. He explained that because "we" (meaning me and him) were part of the base supply system and lived in the supply company barracks but were not assigned directly to the 351st supply squadron, that we were basically on our own: no brass to look over our shoulder or bother us. We had our own office and a tool crib that held special tools the civilians could sign out to work on the missiles and such. We made our own schedule and kept a low profile, away from everyone, because no one really knew where we belonged.

There was another office, through a doorway, next to ours. It was manned by two top Sergeants. Man, they had an awful lot of stripes on their sleeves and had been "around" as the saying goes. Senior Master Sergeant Zertuch and Staff Sergeant Clark were their handles, as best as I can recall. They were not assigned to the supply squadron so we had no contact with them outside our duty station. If Whit and I weren't around, they would cover for us. I'll tell you, looking back, that had to be one of the best assignments of the whole squadron. We even had authority to order any item for any reason for any use due to the fact that we had Top Secret Clearance as a result of the importance of the status of the missiles. If only I knew then what I know now. Well, we were young and more importantly, both Whit and I were honest. We never really abused the system.

One of the best things I loved about my job was the fact I could fly in the choppers out to the missile sites anytime I wanted. After all, I had to keep track of the maintenance being done on them with our tools. It was great. I flew every opportunity I had. I loved the choppers and learned everything I could about them. They were the famous Huey models that were so well known in Vietnam. I got to know all the pilots very well.

Chapter 3

On one particular day, there was just me and the pilot going out. I remember that we flew out to one site and dropped off a package, and the pilot asked me if I wanted a cup of coffee. I said, "Sure." He couldn't shut the chopper down, so he stayed with the bird and I went into the missile site for two cups of coffee. I knew enough that when around a chopper, caution is the name of the game. First and foremost, you never, *ever* walk behind the bird. That is due to the tail rotor. That rotor spins so fast you can't see it to judge the distance you are from it. You could actually walk right into it without any warning, and then you would be dead. So the common practice is to walk in front of the bird, where the pilot can see you and the main rotor is high enough that it can't hit you. So I got two coffees, but not full, because even at idle the main blades give such a powerful down wash of air that it will blow a full cup of coffee all over the place.

Well, mission complete. We had our break and headed back to base. I wish that coffee was the highlight of the flight, but when we were coming in for a hover landing, something went drastically wrong. There wasn't any conversation between me and the pilot, but we made a very hard landing. Later, I found out it was called settling with power. It's about the same thing that happens when an airplane loses lift on the wings and can't fly or stay airborne. Well, it was a very hard landing. We dropped about 20 feet. I was in the back troop seat and on my headset I heard the pilot say "Shit!" and we hit Mother Earth. The skids took the shock and we bounced up like mad and rolled to the right. I thought for sure we were going over on our side, but we didn't.

The second time we hit the ground, the main rotor flexed down and cut off the tail boom. "What a ride," I thought. We spun around, but maybe not. One thing about a chopper is that you just can't bail out unless the main rotor has stopped. If it hasn't, chances are you could be cut in half as long as something is spinning over you. It probably only took a couple of seconds, but it seemed like a long time. We bailed out of that bird fast after everything stopped turning. Man, what a mess.

Nothing really came of the crash because it was determined that something mechanical happened to the chopper. Even after all of that, I still thought those Hueys were a great, safe chopper to fly in. After all, no one had a scratch. I still flew and wasn't bothered by what happened. It is strange, but before the crash, everyone I knew wanted me to get them a ride in a chopper. After the crash, no one ever bothered me again about it. Life resumed the normal routine again.

About a week after the crash (later termed a "hard landing"), a huge transport, well huge for the period, called a Globemaster, was doing touch and go practice landings at our base. I guess it was from a reserve outfit somewhere. A touch and go landing was when an aircraft comes down on the runway for a landing, but instead of stopping, they keep going down the runway and take off again. It is a common practice for all pilots as they build up hours and train in landings. Well anyway, this plane was one of the older types with four huge propellers on it. It was very big and could haul trucks and the like. The front opened up with two big doors and ramps came out for the load. I think it was empty as this was just practice flying. The plane came in and touched down then took off again, but this time, for some reason, it only made it about a mile out from the base and then it crashed and burned in a field.

I don't know if anyone was killed or not, but when I went out to see the wreckage the next day, I couldn't see how anyone could have gotten out alive. It was completely burned. The Military Police were there guarding it so no one could get too close. I think that is another reason the "hard landing" of the week prior was overlooked so fast.

Another good thing about my duty station was that if there was a wartime alert, like a nuclear attack on-base or a drill, all supply squadron personnel were required to report to the base supply area. So that is where I would go according to orders. Once there, everyone would have an assigned post or duty; everyone, that is except for me. After all, I was "Spare Parts." No one knew what to do with me. And thankfully, before any shit detail could be found for me one of my buddy sergeants from the adjoining office would call supply squadron headquarters and request me at my duty station, where I was needed.

And because it was wartime conditions and they just couldn't be driving a pee-on like me around, I'll never forget how the supply section had to go through channels to get me special transportation to my duty station. But, I was needed at my duty station. Talk about feeling important; not even the base commander could move around. But, Airman 3rd class Stoddard could. And when I reported to my duty station there were two smiling sergeants that just said they just didn't think it would be right to let those supply people take advantage of my good nature. I'll never forget the kindness and thoughtfulness Sergeants Zertuch and Clark afforded me in those times: really great guys.

Other than the alerts we had, once in a while my duty station was just like a civilian job. I worked 8 hours at my duty station, then closed up shop and could do whatever I wanted until 07:00 hours the next morning. I'd go back to the barracks, chow, and then hang around. There was a movie theater on base and sometimes I'd go to the movies. Believe me; I saw a lot of movies. Well, one evening, I was standing in line for a ticket and a top Sergeant I knew from another squadron came by and we started talking. He said he ran the movie projectors at the theater for extra cash and asked me if I was interested in doing the same. I said, "Sure." And I was taught how to run the big movie projectors.

In those days, the film for a movie consisted of huge reels of film. There were two projectors and the reels were numbered so you knew which to start with. Toward the end of the reel, a cue called a "hickey" showed on the screen. That little "hickey" was a spot that always appeared in the lower corner of the picture on the screen. But only for a second or two. That first one, then another. People watching the show usually never even noticed them. Well, those cues meant that a scene change was coming up and the reel was just about done. So, during the scene change, you dropped a shutter on the first projector and started the second projector. And, if your timing was right, people would never know you had switched projectors. Then, you had to pull the reel off the first projector, put the reel in a rig and rewind it by hand so that it would be at its starting point for the next showing. After doing that, you put the third reel on the first projector to be prepared to swap it back from projector two at the end of that reel. It sounds complicated, but it worked out pretty good, and after you have seen the movie a couple of times, you knew when the "hickeys" were coming up and it went very well.

The worst problems in working in the projection were: number one, you were alone, number two, the light for the camera was generated by a type of welding spark and you had to adjust the rod for maximum light and if you weren't paying attention, the light and film on the screen would get dark, and the most embarrassing thing was if the guy running the booth or film before you didn't rewind the film, that meant when you started the film, it was backwards. Boy, the audience sure would let you know when you screwed up. To this day, when I'm watching an old movie, even on TV, I can pick up on the hickeys when they come up. I worked at the theater off and on for about four months.

Chapter 4

The barracks was a reasonable place to live. They were two stories high, made out of cement blocks, and set up like a building for bachelors. None of us were married and it was two men to a room. My roommate was an airman, like me, and was in my training flight at Lackland, Texas. His name was Daniel J. Brady from New Jersey. He was a short man, about 5 feet 4 inches I would guess, and when I signed into the Supply Squadron Bks number 1433, I was told he had requested me as a roommate. Why? I don't know. I never asked him. Well D.J., as he became known, turned out to be a great guy. His mouth made up for his size, but he never insulted anyone or made any enemies. He was well liked and had a great sense of humor. We got along great. I wouldn't have wanted another roommate.

Each two man room had two single cots with a desk in between and stand up lockers a few feet off the end of your rack. The room also had two dressers and a sink. The bathroom in the middle of the building was a community type affair and two men were assigned morning duty for one week to keep it spotless. On the first floor, there was a laundry room with washers and dryers and we all did our own laundry and ironing. We also had sewing kits and did our own uniform repair. Also on the first floor were the squadron admin section and the First Sergeant's Office. The First Sergeant was a position given to a higher ranking Sergeant in the unit. He was the go between the enlisted personnel and the officer in charge of the company. Every outfit had a first Sergeant. He just about ran the outfit and took care of the everyday problems that came up before they got to the officer in charge or the OIC. You had to make your rack every morning and your room had to be clean and neat at all times. Once or twice a month, everyone in the barracks had to take part in what was called a field day, only it wasn't in the day, but in the evening, after work, and the whole place had to be washed and all floors including your room had to buffed and brought to a high shine. Being that we were all living together and the place was always super clean anyway, it made keeping it clean easy.

Also in the barracks was a room called the day room. It had padded chairs and a T.V. set. The day room could hold just about 40 guys at one time to watch T.V. or have a bull session. It was in this day room one evening that the great Snipe Hunt was hatched. I had got to know some of the guys in the barracks, especially the guys in the rooms around mine. Some had been on-base for some time and we became pretty good friends.

One night, we all were sitting around talking and one of the guys brought up a "snipe" hunt as something to do. So it was asked by the new guys, me included, what exactly a snipe hunt was. Well apparently, there is a bird in Missouri called a snipe. It doesn't fly and runs around at night looking for worms and such to eat. It is about the size of a small chicken. Well, one of the guys said you catch them at night with a bag and flashlight. It seems one or two guys go into the woods. After the guy with the light and bag finds a good spot to sit and wait, the guys in the brush stomp around and make some noise causing the snipe to run. He won't fly at night because he can't see that well in the dark. So to catch the bird, the hunter with the bag and light sets up. All he has to do is hold the bag open on the ground and shine the light into the bag. The bird sees the opening and runs in it to hide. Simple.

Well, I didn't believe these guys. So I came up with a dictionary and looked up snipe. Well, low and behold, there on page 855 of my Webster's Desk Dictionary was the definition of snipe: a long billed game bird, found in marshy areas; also to shoot at someone from a concealed position. Well, there is a snipe, so I was in on the hunt. We all had Class A passes to the base so we could all come and go anytime. There were six of us when we left the base for the great hunt. I can't remember who had the car, but we piled in and were on our way. It must have been about 10 at night with a new moon. It was a perfect night for hunting snipe, we were told. Two other new guys and myself had the bags and flashlights as we didn't know the woods and the other three would drive the snipes in.

The three of us with lights were dropped off about 200 feet apart and walked off the road a short distance. I found a nice comfortable clearing that I thought would be perfect and settled in with bag and flashlight at the ready. I heard the three drivers, as they were called; pull the car over where they then got out making a wide circle to drive the birds in. Right about then I started to notice how bad the bugs were in the woods by the swamps. I wish I had brought some bug juice with me. I could hear the drivers start the drive. They were noisy as all get out. As time went by and they got closer, it seemed that there wasn't as much yelling and stomping as I thought there'd be, but more laughter and cat calls. Then I heard something very strange. It got very quiet. I listened, got my light ready, and then it happened; I heard the car that brought us scrub out and drive away. My friends and I were left holding the bag: no snipes and no ride back to base. It was a lot of laughter now that I think of it. The three hunters got together and started walking for what seemed like an hour, but in reality, it was probably closer to 20 minutes before our buddies came back and picked us up. The joke was on us, but now we were one of the team. I'll always remember the Snipe Hunt and smile every time I do.

Chapter 5

After about three months, my good friend Whit got his wish in the form of a transfer. It wasn't exactly what he had in mind, but a transfer anyhow. He had thoughts of Germany or maybe Japan, but when you request a transfer in the service, you go where they send you. Well, no glory for Sergeant Whitaker; he was ordered to Korea. Not a pleasant place, but you just say, "Yes, sir!" and pack your bags. But, knowing Whit, I'm sure he was a credit to whatever outfit he ended up in.

After Whit left, the section known as Consolidated Line Maintenance Supply Point became one lonely place. About two weeks after he'd left, I heard that the base was starting a ceremonial drill team to represent the base in parades, weddings, funerals, and any other function that could represent the base. Well, for some reason, I really liked spit and polish outfits, so I volunteered for the team. I went through the process of marching tests and following orders, and somehow I was appointed to the Whiteman Air Force Base Drill Team.

Well, let me tell you, being appointed and drilling in public are two different things. It takes a lot of hard work before it all falls into place. I think we trained for up to four or five hours every evening for a month before we were issued our rifles, and what a thrill it was when it started to all fall into place. The weapons we had were the famous M-1 Garand rifles, with bayonets. That, to me, is the best all-around balanced gun to use in a drill team, especially when you do what is called the "Queen Anne Salute." In this salute, you have to throw the rifle into the air where it spins 360 degrees and as you catch it on the way down, you kneel with the rifle held by your right side. It just worked perfect with that weapon, and it had to or you were out of the team. A person couldn't screw up. It had to be perfect.

We got to be very good and traveled all over putting on shows. We learned a lot of things, like you never want to be near a band because you can't hear the commands over the band music, or never march behind a mounted unit because you still have to march straight and true. I loved the drill team and all the travel and people we met. I stayed on the team until I was transferred.

Right after I joined the drill team, I got a new boot to break in. I showed him the ropes and what was expected of him, but he had a very bad attitude. At first I thought it was me, but through the staff sergeants, I found out that this new boot I had, named Maxwell, was assigned to me because he didn't fit in anywhere else. He had the attitude of a draftee and didn't give a damn about a thing. He just didn't care, but we made it work somehow.

I was the boss and had about a years' time in grade over him, but only three months later, he was promoted to Airman 2nd Class. That promotion put him over me and that made him the boss of my section. All the staff sergeants I knew protested but to no avail. When that happened, I kind of got a bad attitude. The first thing I did was request a transfer out of the unit. I went through channels as required, right up to the squadron commander. I can't remember if he was a Colonel or a Major, but I do remember he wasn't very happy. I was ordered to stay where I was, so I immediately put in for another transfer. Then waited.

Just about the only enjoyment for me during this period was the drill team and when not involved with the team, on weekends I was going to Kansas City. You see, the base ran a bus leaving the USO (United Service Organizations) building Saturday morning and went directly to the USO building in Kansas City, and then back to the base Sunday afternoon free of charge to all base personnel. I sure looked forward to the trip to K.C (as everyone called Kansas City). It was on one of those weekends in K.C. that I became a Turtle, or I should say, a member of the Turtle Club. I was in a bar with some other G.I.s from just about all the branches of the service (except the Navy and Coast Guard, didn't see many of those branches in K.C.).

We were all talking and this one guy from the Air Force says to a couple of us, "Hey are any of you guys Turtles?"

Well, we all look at each other like this guy has lost it. So one guy responds, "You bet your sweet ass I am."

Well, that gets the rest of us talking and asking questions. It turns out that there is an international association of TURTLES. It is a club that has no meetings, no dues, and seems to be recognized worldwide. Well, no dues? Count us in! How do you join? Come to find out a person has to take a test and pass to get into the "Turtle Club".

"What kind of a test," we asked?

And, we were told it was just four questions and you could be a member. I was for it, along with some of the other guys.

First, we were told we had to think only clean thoughts to answer the questions, and clean thoughts only. That seemed strange to hear for a bunch of G.I.s. We were all separated to be asked the questions alone, so our answers couldn't be heard by the others.

My turn came and question one was asked, "What is it a man can do standing up, a woman sitting down, and a dog on three legs?"

"That is easy," I replied. "Take a leak."

Buzz, wrong answer. I wasn't keeping clean thoughts.

Okay, I'll come back to it. What is question number two?

"What is it that a cow has four of and a woman has only two of?"

Okay. "Breasts," I answer.

Buzz, wrong answer again!

Okay, I'm getting the hang of this. Not clean thoughts, right?

Question three: "What is a four letter word ending in 'K' that means the same thing as intercourse?"

I know--clean thoughts. I've had enough I answer that I don't know. How about question four?

"What is on a man that is round and hard and sticks so far out of his pajamas you can hang a hat on it?"

Well I had an answer, but I knew it would be wrong, so I just said "I give up."

I asked if there was any way to pass the test, and he said, "Sure, I'll tell you the answers". He said, "Number one: Shake hands. Numbers two: Legs. Number three, answer is: Talk. Number four: His head. You are now a member of the Turtle Club. Govern yourself accordingly and procure new members. And one more thing I was told, it is assumed that all prospective Turtles own a Jack Ass. This assumption is the reason for the password. The password must be given if you are ever asked by a fellow member, "Are you a turtle?" You must then reply,"You bet your sweet ass I am." If you do not give the password in full, because of embarrassment or some other reason, you forfeit a beverage of your choice. So always remember the password. I was now an official member of the Turtle Club. I even received a membership card with the test and answers on the back, very impressive to say the least.

Chapter 6

Nineteen sixty five was a year to remember. About five weeks later, the trips to K.C. all ended with a bang, only about three months after they started. I should say rather with a crash, and one I will never forget. I was riding in the right front seat and talking to the military driver. The bus was the civilian version of a school bus and I remember the driver was saying that there seemed to be something strange with the steering, but everything was going fine. Just as we entered the outskirts of K.C. on the divided highway, I think it was Rte. 70, all hell broke loose. The bus started swerving very sharply across the lanes of the highway. The driver yelled out that we were going to roll over and I yelled back the same thing. I remember grabbing the pole that was there that went from the floor to the roof of the bus right as the steps to the doorway start. I closed my eyes as we started to slide sideways and then rolled onto the right side. We slid a distance, what a racket, and then it was quiet.

It didn't take long and then the bus started to fill with smoke. Now, because the bus was laying on its right side, the door was useless as it was on the ground side. As I said before, this was a typical school bus that had the windows that only opened one half way down, and would you believe I went out through one of those windows, just like about six other guys did when the bus started to fill with smoke. And to show you what military training does to you, when I got out of the bus, I realized I didn't have my cover (hat) on. We all had to travel in uniform and the rule is if you are outside, you have to have your hat on. Well mine was knocked off during the roll. Can you believe, I went back through the window, got my cover and climbed back out? I did. It was just automatic. You don't go outside without your cover. Anyway, everyone survived and we just left the scene. I heard later that the poor driver was made to pay for the bus because the government said he was speeding and the accident was his fault.

Well anyway, after the accident no more trips to K.C. A month later I was promoted to Airman 2nd Class, but Maxwell had more time in grade than I did so he was still boss even though I still ran everything. It could have been worse.

Well, things went along, and then one day Airman Maxwell was gone. He sure did have some pull. By now, I suppose he is either a general somewhere or a lawyer for the civil liberties union, but whatever, he was gone. I then got another boot to break in. The new man, fresh out of basic training, was a very good kid. His last name was Hume, I believe. He was married and lived with his wife in an apartment off base. His home was in St. Louis, Missouri, so he had a chance to get home once in a while; great luck for him. I even got the chance to go home with him and his wife a couple of times to check out the sights of St. Louis, a very nice city. At that time, St. Louis was building the great arch called the Gateway to the West and it was very impressive. We stayed at his folk's house in the city, and I sure had a fun time, as they were a great couple.

Back at the base, things were the same. D.J., my roommate, got married to the girl he was going with when he joined up. She was from New Jersey, so he moved off base to an apartment. One of the guys I knew that lived next to me said he wasn't getting along with his roommate, and asked if he could move in with me. He was a nice guy from Texas. His name was Jerrel Diggs. The problem with his roommate was that Jerrel worked days and his roommate worked nights, so they were always waking each other up when they were trying to sleep. Well I said sure, and he moved in. He was a quiet guy and another great roommate.

My request for a transfer was still active. I had taken a leave and gone home to Massachusetts to see my folks. The girl I was going with when I went in had sent me a "Dear John" letter so I didn't have any ties there except for my family and friends, some female, but nothing binding. I had a motorcycle when I went in and had just left it at home when I left. Well, I rode the bike back to the base after my leave. That is a story in itself, but I made it. With a bike I was able to get off base more and meet some of the locals. I started dating and ended up moving in with a very nice girl named Ann, her divorced mother, younger sister by a year or two and a baby brother. I became the man of the house whether I was ready for something like that or not.

It was right after I started going with Ann that her mother, who was a very sharp lady, suggested that I read a book that she had just finished. It was called <u>Dando Shaft</u> as I recall. The thing that I picked up on for some reason was that the main character signed his name with an exclamation mark. I thought that was kind of neat. After reading the book, I started the habit of signing my own name with an exclamation mark. So, in 1965, I started a trend that has eventually taken me through the justice system to register it as part of my name, and has further caused problems that you could never imagine. To this day, I sign my name with an exclamation mark. It is just normal for me now.

Chapter 7

I would go to work at the base, and then at the end of the day, I would come home to my family just like a civilian. My roommate kept up the room I was assigned to in the barracks, so I didn't have to worry about that. Well, put a red blooded guy, 20 years old, in with three ladies that were good looking. Sure was good for me. It started out slowly at first, but before I knew it, I was sleeping on the living room couch at her house. Ann's bedroom was upstairs in the old colonial house they lived in and the mother's bedroom was off the living room. I don't' know how long she had been divorced, but I guess it had been some time. Her name was Kathy and she was probably in her thirties. A good looking lady. She worked as a secretary at the local college during the day, and two nights a week as a bookkeeper at the local movie theater. Her boyfriend owned a local bar and I'd guess he was in his fifties. I got along very well with her and she didn't' mind me going with her daughter at all. The other daughter was a year or two younger than Ann and had a boyfriend who was a nice guy and had his own car so they were gone a lot. I didn't' hang with him at all. There was something about him being a local and me being in the service, but we did get along.

I was having a good time and Ann and I hit it off well. My challenge started New Year's Eve, 1965. Ann and I had sat and watched the New Year come in and she went upstairs to bed just after midnight. I stripped down to my shorts, threw a blanket over me and lay down on the couch like I'd always done and went right to sleep. It must have been about an hour later that I was woke up by what I figured was an argument between Kathy and her boyfriend out in the kitchen. They were both drunk, which was out of character for her, but I could tell it was pretty heated and he ended up storming out of the house. I was drifting back to sleep when Kathy came into the living room on her way to her bedroom. Halfway across the room she took a header and landed on the floor. I jumped up and helped her. She had a robe on but not much else. Boy, was I naive. I had my arm around her, under her arm and helped her to her bed. Well, maybe I wasn't that naive. I laid her down in her bed and she said, "Well are you just going to play with it or are you going to do something?" That was all it took. I mean, I was just a normal red-blooded male. So, we got very close in a short time. After about an hour, I was back on the couch and fell fast asleep, exhausted you might say. That morning, I hadn't thought about what to do when I got up. I could hear Kathy out in the kitchen and was thinking, "What now??" I had to get up. Well, here goes...

I pulled on my pants and walked out into the kitchen. She stopped doing whatever it was and looked at me. I didn't have a clue as to what to say or do. She spoke first: "About last night...it was just something that happened and I think it should be left behind us." I was just thinking something different, but I said I agreed. The household got up and things went back to normal, or what appeared to be normal. I knew the fire had been lit and that it wasn't going to be left behind.

I must have done something right because about a month later, Kathy announced we were all moving to another house closer to downtown Warrensburg and at the new place, I would have my own bedroom with a doorway between my room and Ann's. Seemed good to me. We went and looked at the two story house with a third story bedroom in a cupola type affair. It was a neat house. Kathy would sleep downstairs in a regular bed in the

47

huge living room. So it worked out that the three bedrooms on the second deck were for me, Ann, and her sister whose room was across from mine, and as she said, my room had a connecting door to Ann's through a closet, which was convenient. The younger brother's bedroom was on the third deck, kind of a neat set up.

We rented a moving truck and the great move went well. I was trying to be the perfect gentleman with the family, but I had to get up very early in the morning to get to the base for work. That meant that while everyone else was fast asleep, I was to wake up Kathy just before I left on my bike for the base. Well, she didn't' seem to mind that I would crawl into bed with her and wake her in ways that people dream of being woken up. It was sure a dream that came true for me. Then, I would leave for the base. What a life. Talk about being lucky. I was living a dream. Ann and I were still as close as ever and that door between our rooms got a lot of use. No wonder I only weighed about 150 pounds and was very tired a lot.

Ann had a job at the ticket booth of the movie theater that her mother worked at and at times at night. I worked as an usher if it was a popular movie and the place was packed. The younger sister was still in school as a senior and she was a good looker. One day, Ann was at work and I was in my room with the door open. I think I was polishing my boots for work and Pat, the sister, came upstairs and walked into her room and left the door open, right across from my door. Well, she started to change clothes right in front of me. I was going to say something, but I couldn't. My heart was in my throat. It was some show and I asked her if she knew I was there. She said, "yes," that she "wasn't stupid." I didn't know what to do or think. That statement could cover a lot of territory and I didn't want to admit anything. She didn't finish dressing and came into my room and asked what I was doing. I had to be honest, so I said I was dreaming of having her for supper. She didn't know what I meant, so I asked her if she was willing to learn. Well, one thing led to another and we both got a great education that day. Now, I really had a problem. I really enjoyed myself, and made sure she was a happy camper also. I figured if I could keep everyone happy and be discreet that I might survive what I had gotten myself into. I was 21 and she was 19 so I wasn't a criminal, but if I kept up my schedule, I would be down to 130 pounds in about a month. So, I chose to stay away from Pat unless she came to me. That kind of put the pressure on her, not me. Well, my weight was dropping. I was in great shape and had a permanent smile on my face. Things were going great. But, nothing lasts forever, good or bad. I had my great duty station on the base, the ladies were outstanding, and then my transfer came through.

Chapter 8

1967—1968

I guess it was May 1967 when I was ordered to report to a base in California for advanced infantry training. I would be allowed 10 days to travel home to Massachusetts to get my affairs in order, then I'd travel to California. Advanced infantry training meant only one thing, and it was that I was headed to Vietnam. That was why I had time to go home and get my affairs in order. I processed out of Whiteman AFB. A few days before I left Whiteman, I was contacted by a special branch of the Military Police. It seems my old duty station had been broken into and some tools were stolen. Seeing I had keys and ran the place for almost two years, they just wanted some ideas as to what might have happened. I really didn't have anything to help them. I signed some papers for them and left for Massachusetts.

At home, everyone knew I was headed to Vietnam. Why else would I be going for advanced combat training? At the base, I never really followed the news or current events. I just knew that there was a small war the country was fighting over there, but not much more than that. My G.I. insurance was already made out to my folks and I had no property other than my bike, which I sold in Missouri before I left. So I enjoyed my short leave and approximately eight days later I arrived in California and went through some special training for combat. This training was required because when I was in basic training, the weapons everyone qualified on were outdated, World War II era, .30 caliber carbines. Now, everyone had to be brought up to speed on the current weapons being used.

I was trained on the new M-16 rifle plus the M-60 machinegun, new hand grenade tactics, and the new weapon, the M-79 grenade launcher. And one other thing, for some reason, I was required to get a military driver's license.

It was at this time that I was called into the base personnel office where a note in my file about all my requests for a transfer to another outfit was noted. Well, they, as the saying goes, made me an offer I couldn't refuse. It was an offer that would change my life. The Lieutenant was working on a pilot program. It seems it was his opinion that the

Air Force was not prepared to fight the type of ground war in Vietnam that was required to keep the bases secure. So he was looking for people to go through advanced combat training so we could become combat liaison officers for mutual support roles in combat situations. After reviewing my background, fitness reports and requests for transfers, in his opinion, I was a good candidate for his program. He offered me a reassignment to the U. S. Marine Corps as an Air Force Non Commissioned officer.

There were conditions to my reassignment. I had to complete the basic training course of the United States Marine Recruit Training Depot San Diego, California, and successfully complete the Marine Corps NCO School at Los Pulgas, California. If I agreed and was successful, I would be promoted to the grade of E-4 (Sergeant) and would be transferred at the pleasure of the Government to an overseas duty station.

Do the words "never volunteer" sound familiar? Well, I agreed to the reassignment and its conditions. Talk about a reality check. I never knew how good I had it in the Air Force. But, once a Marine, always a Marine. As I have said before, I really love spit and polish outfits. I found that once you get the routine down, I had already had the basic military procedure from the Air Force. The Marines were just, well let's just say, the real thing. Because I already had two years in and was a Corporal, I was just there to learn the Marine way and the deep shit never hit me too hard.

In the recruit platoon, I wore no rank on my uniform and was just another "Shit Bird." As far as everyone else was concerned, I was just another recruit. We trained on combat situations and I added the .50 Caliber Machine Guns to my qualifications of weapons that "ma deuce," as it is known, is impressive. I was also trained on the United States Rifle, 7.62 Cal M14 Marine combat rifle. I loved to shoot and became a marksman. It is a great rifle and replaced the M-1 Garand that I had been so familiar with. The Marines know what they are doing and are in a class by themselves, head and shoulders above anyone else.

Then I was off to Los Pulgas. That was not like recruit training, but more leadership, military bearing, and Marine Corps history. And through all this, I never saw that Officer from the personnel outfit once. *Now* I knew why he was smiling as I said "Yes."

In the month of September I received orders to report to the Civilian Airport outside San Francisco. I can't remember its name, but there was a section there for military personnel and I had to report in. It was some place. I don't know who ran it, matter of fact, I don't think anyone knew. I gave my orders to a lieutenant and he gave me a number and said I would be called when a space was available on a plane going to Vietnam. My number was for a cot behind a curtain that divided the room we were in into two rooms. I was given two paper sheets and a paper pillow case. No one knew how long it would be before I was called. Behind the curtain, I settled in with about 20 other military people from just about every branch of the services. We had meal chits for a small cafeteria down the hall. We were told not to leave due to the fact our name could be called at any time.

Chapter 9

My orders said I was to report to Saigon, Vietnam MACV. That stands for Military Advisory Command Vietnam. My reporting date was 15 September 1967. The problem was it looked like I wasn't going to leave the States until after that date. I waited and waited at the airport. After a couple of days, I had the system figured out. So one day, I hitched a ride into San Francisco and toured the city. It was a beautiful place for a country boy like me to see. I got back in the early evening and was never missed.

Everyday everyone would get clean paper sheets and pillowcases. In our little sleeping area, they continued calling numbers all day and all night. People would come and go. Sleep wasn't very good for anyone. After about five days, I heard my name called. I couldn't believe it. I was going to be on my way, except, there was a big problem. Well, to me it was a big problem. I was going over on a civilian airplane and the plane wasn't going to Saigon, Vietnam. Oh, it was going to the Nam O.K., but not where I was supposed to be going.

In typical military fashion I was informed that their job was only to get me to the Nam. It was my job to get to my assignment after I got there. Oh boy! I was further informed that the U.S. Marines served 13 months in country, not the standard 12 of all the other units. And even further, that my time in country didn't start until I reported to my assignment. Ugh! Well, off I went. The first stop was the great Hawaiian Islands. It sure was beautiful. I wish I had more time to sightsee, but I only had enough time to buy some cards and see the airport. From there, it was a straight shot to the place that became known as "the Nam" as anyone who was there called it.

I recall landing in the Nam in the late afternoon. The heat was oppressive. We were to deplane and report to an officer, an Army NCO, and show our orders. From there, I went to a small cage and had to turn in all American money I had. I can't remember if I was given local money or if instead I was given what was called MPCs. MPC stood for Military Payment Certificates and was also commonly known as "funny money." It looked something like the bills used in the game of Monopoly. I wasn't given the chance to eat, but was shown to a tent for visiting or transit troops. I was the only guest, so I had my pick of the several cots inside.

I changed out of my Class A uniform used for travel and put on my utilities; the Air Force calls them fatigues. I was told to sleep fully dressed and shown where the mortar shelter was. It was about 20:30, (8.30 p.m.) so I started a letter home and was sound asleep about 30 minutes later. I don't know what time it was, but I woke up to the loudest damn bang I had ever heard. Little did I know, but the transit tent was right in front of the base artillery unit. I think they planned it that way. I didn't go to the shelter because as I started out, I figured it out, because everything else was quiet. Well, I guess it was welcome to "The Nam."

I was up at about 06:00 the next morning and found the mess tent had some powdered eggs and toast. They even had milk. I thought it strange that I was from another unit and all I had to do was sign in and get chow; no questions asked. After chow, I reported to the orderly room and spoke to the First Sergeant. If the outfit, any outfit, has a good First Sergeant, it sure makes things a lot easier for everyone. This outfit had a good first shirt.

I was advised to grab a convoy going south to what was called Long Binh. It was a main supply depot for the Army, and it was also the Military Jail. It was called "LBJ," for Long Binh Jail, but by happy circumstance, it was also the initials of the President of the United States of America, Lyndon Baines Johnson. The convoy I was in had about 20 trucks, all of which were called "6-bys" or "deuce and a halves." There were some larger 5 ton trucks in with us as well. All were open cabs with no canvas tops, and the truck I was on, which was about the third from the front, had its troop seats down. Troop seats are just wooden slats that run along the side of the body of the truck. All the rest of the trucks were empty. I noticed that the trucks without machineguns mounted at the cab had armed soldiers riding as guards like the old time stagecoaches of the Old West. The trip was dusty hot and took most of the day, but we had no problems. The biggest worry, I found out, was landmines. But, as I said, we pulled into the huge base at Long Binh all intact.

At Long Binh, I was informed that there was a military bus going to Saigon and to just hop aboard. I grabbed my sea bag and got on the bus. There were some other new guys on board so we talked. One topic brought up was the bus we

59

were in. It was like a school bus back in the states, only with military colors and the strange thing was that it had thick wire mesh over the windows. It was the same type of bus that I was in going to KC back in the states that had rolled over. So here I was, in what was supposed to be a hostile country, and was wondering how I could get out of this bus if something happened. I didn't like being penned in, that was, until someone told us the screens were there to keep grenades from being thrown through the open windows. That sure was food for thought. If I wasn't already nervous enough, that didn't help matters any.

The trip was uneventful and I got a chance to view some of the scenery and people on the trip. As we entered the outskirts of Saigon, I noticed that if a person, male or female, had to go to the bathroom, they just stepped off the path, road or sidewalk they were on and did their duty. No one seemed to care or notice. This sure wasn't Kansas, Toto.

Chapter 10

The bus stopped in Saigon and we were told we were at the Saigon USO building and we could get directions from there to wherever we needed. I was told MACV (Military Assistance Command, Vietnam) was not far away, but that I had to report in as soon as I could for my tour of duty to start. It seemed like I was just on the outskirts of the city, but was told I could walk to the Tan Son Nhut Air Base about a mile or two away. So with sea bag in hand, off I went.

Thinking of that sea bag, some outfits call them duffel bags, but no matter what they are called, if you were in service, you know what I mean when I say those things sure are heavy. They hold all your required uniforms and shoes, rain gear, cold and hot weather gear and anything else you could be issued. Every time I see a movie and see actors walking around with their sea bags like they weigh nothing, I get a good chuckle. Those things are heavy!

Well, I walked up what I was told was Main Street and came right to the main entrance to Tan Son Nhut Air Base. It was wide open. I just walked on-base, no check at the gate or anything. I noticed some Vietnamese soldiers and Military Police there, but they were just waving everyone through. I sure thought that was strange . I just couldn't get over how lax security was for being in what I thought was a war zone. I guess this wasn't going to be as bad of a gig as I had thought. I was a little confused and walked around a while, but that damn sea bag was just too heavy. I asked a couple of G.I.s how to get to MACV, and they told me to hail a cab and he would take me there for about a buck. So I yelled at a passing cab. I just couldn't believe all the traffic that was traveling around on this base. I mean, there were a lot of military vehicles of all types, but also cabs, motorbikes, some kind of three-wheeled moped type things, bicycles and everything else you could think of. The cab I ended up in was a small car with the engine in the rear, about the size of the old VW Bug.

The driver let me out in front of MACV and *now* I was impressed with some security. It made me want to buy stock in a barbwire company. Everything was protected and sand bagged. There were guard posts everywhere. I was led into a room to meet with an Army NCO (non-commissioned officer). I showed him my orders and he kind of went blank. This was something he knew nothing about. He left and I waited. There was air conditioning and it felt good. He came back in and said that I was supposed to be with Third Marines in I Corps but that wasn't what the Air Force had in mind. The Third Marines were up north in Da Nang, also known as "Dodge City." I was in Saigon. All I knew was that I wanted to get signed "in country" so that my time would start to count down towards the end of my tour. The Sergeant agreed and said he would get everything squared away.

Well, after about a dozen phone calls, I was told to report back to Tan Son Nhut Air Base. I was going to be assigned to the 371st Combat Support Group. I would be assigned further out of that outfit. The Sergeant got me a ride back to TSN Air Base. I was directed to a closet-sized office to see a Major. He stated he didn't know what to do with me, but he would let me know. Some more phone calls and another Sergeant (Air Force) took me to a barracks where I was given a locker to stow my gear. The Sergeant was the first guy to ask me why I was wearing a Marine utility cap. I tried to explain what was going on and he just shook his head and laughed. He said, "Didn't you ever learn not to volunteer?"

The Barracks I was in was what is called "hooch." It had wooden slats about 4 inches apart halfway up the sides and just a screen the rest of the way up to the roof. It was about 40 feet long, had screen doors at each end, and was lined with bunk beds on each side of the center aisle. The lockers were the metal, two-door stand up type with a hasp to secure the door with a padlock. I was on the bottom bunk. There was no one on the top bunk, but the locker next to mine had a padlock on it so I figured it was claimed and in use. The Sergeant said that an officer would be contacting me in a day or two and set me up. In the meantime, I was on my own.

The mess hall was about a mile or so away (what a huge base this was!) and I could eat after signing in. Well, at last I was in country and my time clock was ticking. I went to the chow hall. It looked like a new building. It was the metal prefab type and was a good size, probably close to one hundred feet long with entrance doors on each end with the kitchen in the middle. All I had to do was sign in under my unit assignment, grab a tray and follow the line to the serving stations. It was just like back in the states. The food was good and they had fresh milk or water to drink; all you wanted. On each table was a small bowl filled with large orange pills. I was told that they were malaria pills and everyone was required to take one on the same day once a week. There were also salt pills for anyone who wanted them. The people serving the food onto the plates on our trays were all Vietnamese. This was the only difference, other than the pills, that I could see between this place and a State side chow hall.

After chow, I decided to walk around and see the base. I learned that a movie theater was being built along with a Post Office and Base Exchange. It seemed to be building up just like a new base in the States. All the new buildings were of the metal prefabricated type. The other buildings, such as the administration and base squadron buildings, seemed to be old cement whitewashed buildings from the French colonial era. Most of the roads on-base were hot top, but everything was very dusty. As I walked around, I saw that there was even a club where the enlisted men on-base could go to and drink. This sure was a nice place.

Well, after walking around for a couple of hours, I went back to my hooch, and when I got back, I met the Airman who had the rack above mine. I don't remember his name, but I do remember he worked at the bomb dump on the Air Base. He was a nice kid. He gave me the basic lowdown on what was going on and where the mail room was so I could get setup with mail. This base was huge and the Mail room was just a square building with small post office mail boxes all over the outside you got a number for a box and a small padlock to put on it and you got your Mail there anytime you wanted. The next day, I was informed I had to get a Vietnamese driver's licenses to add to my military licenses so I could drive in country. Believe me, I had no plans to drive in Vietnam, but I didn't know what Uncle Sam had in store for me. So I was told where to report and said, "Yes, sir," to the Staff Sergeant who told me to go get my license and reported to the school.

The school building was an old house trailer, about 30 feet long, with an office and school room in it. It was set right beside the road, just inside the main gate to the base. I was given a book to study and then I had to take a test on the road signs and language. The first time I flunked, so back to the book I went. A few days later, I passed, and was then qualified to drive in country. <u>What I didn't know, but I had the licenses. (?)</u>

Chapter 11

One thing bothered me; the base that I was on was wide open. Traffic just came and went: civilian and military. It was supposed to be a warzone and you would never know it. No one had a weapon, except on the gate. There were a few bunkers made of sandbags on-base, and there were even Vietnamese civilian houses on-base. They were just shacks really, but they were all over the place. Outside on the streets of Saigon, everything was sandbagged and guarded by all sorts of armed guards. Those street guards had every type of weapon you could think of. I mean, from new M-16s to old M-1 Garands, and the M-1 Carbine to the old 45 cal Thompson machine gun. What a hodgepodge of weapons and bunkers and barbwire everywhere. It was like everything was backwards; outside the base there were all kinds of security and on-base, nothing. It was just weird.

Sometime in October, I was advised by the officer I had met on the first day in Saigon that I was to be assigned to the inspection section, so I could have the freedom to go to further training as it came up. "What Training?" I asked. I was told I would be advised at a later time. I was to report to a Staff Sergeant with a long, Polish name that was running the inspection section. Upon reporting to the Senior Master Sergeant (I'll call him Ski,) I found a man that was not very happy to get me. I was informed that he was told I was "spare parts" and would be assigned only on paper to him, and furthermore, that even though I only had Corporal stripes on, my Staff Sergeant orders were en route. That sure pleased me when I heard it. So in turn, I was assigned to another Senior Master Sergeant named Conrad. The Staff Sergeant, or rather Senior Master Sergeant Conrad, would be my boss while on-base. Senior Master Sergeant Ski didn't want me in his section, so I was to report to Senior Master Sergeant Conrad on the flight line every day for inspection duties. That was okay with me.

It was about this time that when I was walking back from chow one day, that an Air Force Police Officer stopped me and said I was out of uniform because I was wearing a Marine cover with an Air Force uniform. My orders didn't matter. I was informed that the news media ran the show around the base and everyone had to have the same uniform on so that they looked correct. I couldn't believe what I was hearing, but in service, you never argue with the military police. I had to get an Air Force hat, and I did.

Two weeks later I got my orders promoting me to Sergeant. To me, that meant #1. the lieutenant in California kept his word and #2. I got a pay raise. Furthermore, a week later I was advised I couldn't stay in the barracks I was in because now, I was a Non-Commissioned Officer and had to move to the NCO barracks to fit my status. Gee, I was coming up in the world. My new hooch, # 818, was small, with only about 15 guys in it. There were no bunk beds and everyone had their own small cubical. We also had a TV and a refrigerator; not bad. I had the chance to move in with the Navy detachment a couple of hooches over, but under the assignment of the 3rd Marines, and even though the Marines were the better part of the Navy, I knew better. It didn't take me long to learn though that if I wanted good chow or a cold drink, the Navy always had anything you wanted...for a price. They had simply everything brought in from shipboard and sold it to us grunts. They sure made a lot of cash. They even had cold Coca-Cola. What a treat. The swabs were okay, and they sure had great stuff. I wonder where all the money they made went.

My new rank put me in a whole new world. The new barracks were good and no one bothered me. Everyone else in the hooch was the same rank as I was. In talking with them, I learned that just about all of them worked in what was called P.O.L. which stood for Petroleum, Oil, and Lubricants. Mostly what they did was refuel all the planes that came and went at the base. Let me tell you, that was one busy bunch of guys. They were all good hard workers from all over the states. None were from Massachusetts. I remember George Rice from Talladega, Alabama and another from Pottsville, Pennsylvania and one from Gorham, Maine. The guy from Maine, I don't remember his name, but for some reason I have his address written on the inside of my helmet.

For some reason, I was the only guy in the hooch that had any regular combat training. A few of the guys were kind of suspicious of me, thinking that I was some kind of undercover cop or something. They always commented on not knowing where I worked, and how I seemed to come and go as I pleased. I gave a halfhearted explanation to them, but it didn't go over well. Their suspicions only grew stronger when after the conversation with them; I kind of disappeared a short time later for a couple of weeks. They also had brought up the fact that the first Sergeant that ran the company knew me, but I didn't know him.

One day, about two weeks after my promotion, the First Sergeant called me into his office and told me I would be going TDY (military jargon for "temporary duty assignment") to a base not far from TSN, a place called Cu Chi. There, I would learn about the guerilla tactics the Viet Cong were using against us. It seems a tunnel system had been discovered on this base and the system was being used to train U.S. soldiers how to detect and destroy enemy tunnel systems.

I had learned from talking with other guys and observing the military trucks on the base, that most outfits had pet names for their vehicles. In this case, I was told I could get my gear and hop onto any truck that had "Cu Chi Express" on it. The vehicles were so named due to the fact that they had to run the "gauntlet" of a road to get to the base of Cu Chi. You see, the base was very secure due to its size, but the road in was not secure and was always a problem. I informed the Sergeant that I didn't even have a weapon or combat gear yet. He told me to go to BEMO (Base Equipment Management Office) and sign out anything I required. Well, at least I could now get the combat gear I needed. I simply found a doorway that said BEMO and went in. All I had to do was tell them what I wanted; a field pack, M-16, 400 rounds of ammo, a flack vest, a couple of canteens, web gear and for good measure, I even got a new pair of combat boots. These were a new type with drain holes for water and canvas uppers for ventilation. They also had a fiberglass insole so when the wearer stepped on spikes (sharpened bamboo poles), they wouldn't penetrate your boot and then your foot (or, rather, they *shouldn't*).

I got everything I wanted signed my name and went back to my hooch to pack. Some of the guys in my hooch were kind of wondering what was going on, but I didn't take the time to explain. This was a decision I would later regret. I packed light, secured my locker and went out to the main base road. The base was so big that it was bad manners not to stop for a G.I. when he held his hand up for a ride. I spotted a Cu Chi Express marked truck and held my hand up and it stopped. It was a standard deuce and a half and was headed to run the gauntlet in to Cu Chi.

There was only the driver and a gunner manning an M-60 machinegun on the door post. I jumped up into the bed and settled in by some boxes in the bed. I could talk to the guys in front, and I told them I was going the distance to Cu Chi. They were glad to have another gun on board. I asked them what was in the boxes, and they answered "air conditioners," of all things. We figured they were for the officers, as us grunts didn't have anything like that. I was told that there were two more trucks waiting for us by the gate out of Tan Son Nhut so we would ultimately be a three truck convoy. We would be the last truck; not a bad spot.

Chapter 12

The gate we left by was like a back door. We traveled by the base Post Office and a new building that was being put up. I heard it was going to be the new Base Exchange or BX, as they were called. The BX was the base store where you would go to purchase your everyday needs plus trinkets, kind of like a Wal-Mart. The U.S. Government was trying to bring daily life as it was back in the States, to Vietnam.

The three trucks were waved through the gate and out onto the dirt road to Cu Chi. We were third in our little convoy. We went by a textile mill and after a while, into a forest-like area. It could have been a rubber plantation. Anyway, it was all trees. The driver and gunner were not from Massachusetts, so the conversation was about things in general and time in country. None of us were short timers, meaning you only had a month or so to go before your time in country was up.

Everything was going fine when the truck in front of us just blew up. The whole thing went about five feet into the air then came back down. Our truck slid to a stop because the road was blocked and the gunner started spraying the area with the machine gun and then signaled me to do the same. I don't think they were too impressed with me because I was so slow to react. After about 5 minutes, we stopped shooting. By then, the dust had cleared and everything was quiet. We stayed hunkered down for a couple of minutes and nothing happened. There was some talk that if it had been an RPG (rocket propelled grenade), we would have been hit already, and with no shooting coming in at us, it had to be a mine and not an ambush, thank God. The gunner stayed on his gun and the driver and I got out to check on the truck in front. The first truck was okay also and backed up to us. The driver and gunner in the truck that blew up were shaken up but, unbelievably, were okay. The rear tandem wheels and axles were blown off the truck, but the front was still together. There was a big hole in the road where the mine had exploded. The amazing thing was that the first truck passed right over it and it didn't go off, but the second truck did set it off somehow. I learned fast that it was just what is called "the fall of the cards." Either you are lucky, or you are not.

Well, no one was injured except for some blood coming out of our ears. I don't think it was 10 minutes before there were two choppers over us as an air net. I figured the first truck had a radio and had called in. The truck I was in was told to stay to guard the damaged vehicle with the choppers until a support team with a wrecker showed up. I went in the first truck with the driver and gunner of truck two. I felt bad leaving them there, but with the choppers overhead, they would be fine. About 15 minutes after we left the scene, we met an armored personnel carrier, a wrecker and a truck full of troops going to the scene. I felt better after that. After we pulled into Cu Chi, we had to fill out an after action report. I had never seen one, so I let the other guys do it. I guess after being in country for a while, it was just another day's work for the truckers. I was thinking that I had a lot to learn in a hurry, but now, I was with an Army unit.

I was informed of where to stay for the tunnel training classes. I would be staying in hooch, only this one was a tent with the sides rolled up. After breakfast the next morning, I reported to another tent set up like a classroom, or more of an introduction center to tunnel warfare. I was very uncomfortable as I was thinking about being stuck in an underground tunnel. I learned just how good the Viet Cong made the tunnels that were being found in our area of operation. The Army had tried every way possible to drive the Viet Cong out of the tunnels when they were found with very poor results. They tried to blow them up, but they were built with a type of baffles in them to prevent total destruction. They tried flooding them, but there wasn't enough water available. They tried CS (2-chlorobenzylidene malononitrile) gas, that is, tear gas, but the tunnels were so long that didn't work very well either. The best way, they found, was to train people to go into the tunnel with a pistol and follow them out. Can you imagine going into a tunnel, full of booby traps and hostile people that will do anything to kill you, with just a flashlight and a pistol? I sure didn't like that idea.

Well, we studied tunnels and all the bad stuff that can be found in them. Then, we went out into the field to find them. We were told what to look for and how to react. It seems the tunnel entrance is usually covered by someone in a foxhole not far away, if not that, then by a booby trap. There were always false openings, dead ends and the like. It was not an easy task, and these were tunnels that had already been found. The first day, we found two out of six; not very good.

The next day, the good luck gods smiled on me again. In class, I was told I would not be a tunnel rat, as those G.I.s were called, that went into the tunnels. You see, at six feet tall, I was simply too big to maneuver in the tunnel, although there were tunnel rats that were taller but they volunteered for the job. Thank you, God. I stayed in the class and learned all I could about punji stakes, pitfalls, trip wires and the like. I sure wasn't smiling as much anymore. This was serious business.

I stayed at Cu Chi for about one week. I can't remember if I celebrated my birthday at Cu Chi or not, for it was right about that time, early November, that I was back at Tan Son Nhut. I reported back to my duty station and the next day a Staff Sergeant from a different outfit asked me if I had the proper driver's licenses to drive in country. Dummy me said, "Yea." So, I found out that I would be taking a box truck north to Long Binh. There would be two gunners in the back and one up front with me. Well, I figured if the government can run buses on this route, I should be able to drive it okay. All I had to do was drive through Saigon, hit the main highway north and go.

Chapter 13

Now, let me tell you, just driving in the Nam is a trip in itself. You see, over there the vehicles have the right of way and not the pedestrians, so in the city, people are charging across the roadway in between cars, trucks, taxis, motorcycles, water buffalo carts, and anything else coming down the road. If you stop you are going to get rammed, or you risk the chance of being shot at. It was almost like highway driving here, only worse there. For the life of me, I don't know why or how I ended up driving a large truck in Vietnam.

The Staff Sergeant in charge rode up front with me. In the back of this box truck was only one gunner with an M-16. One of our gunners didn't show. So, what does that make? One smart guy out of four. So, off we went. The Staff Sergeant with me knew the way. All I had to do was drive. I remember the truck was an International Harvester Co. and had a 5-speed manual transmission. It only had one set of dual tires on the rear axle that made it a six wheel truck, not to be confused by what was known as a 6-by. 6-by was military jargon for a truck that had two axles in the rear and also had all wheel drive to the front, so in bad going, all tires were drive tires. Simply put, all six points where the tires were on the ground were drive tires, thus 6-by. These were also known as deuce and a half trucks because the common cross country load they could carry was two and one half tons. Anyhow, the truck I had did not have all-wheel drive, but I wasn't going off roading, so I didn't need it. The plan was to leave Saigon, get up to Long Binh and back before dark. Only armed convoys traveled after dark, and it was only when they really had to in a dire situation.

Well, we got underway, went out through the main gate at TSN. We didn't even get stopped or checked. I'll never understand the lack of security at that base. I joined the mass of traffic going through Saigon. I believe that at that time, everyone in that huge city owned a motorbike. On the other side of the city were the docks with all the ships unloading and waiting to be unloaded. We crossed the bridge going out of the city out to what I believe was highway one. All the bridges were very well protected either by bunkers, barbed wire and gun emplacements, or by tanks. I tried to keep my speed up because it is harder to hit a faster vehicle.

It was an uneventful ride to Long Binh. I was driving but had no idea why we were there or what we were picking up. I was just a driver. I parked the truck where I was told and the gunner in back and the Staff Sergeant in charge went off to pick up some stuff, so I was free to walk around. This was another huge base. I was looking for the prison because I was curious, but didn't find it, but I did find something a lot better.

In those days in service we didn't have the fancy meals they call MREs (meals ready to eat) today. We had the same C-rations that were used in WWII and Korea. They came with their own can opener, called a P-38, and everyone I knew carried their own P-38 with them, as did I. I still have mine. I just couldn't imagine having a can of C-rations and no way to open it. Anyhow, everything we ate in the field came out of small cardboard boxes in which were a couple of small cans, some brown tinfoil covered biscuits or crackers, some peanut butter or other small type of snack, two pieces of gum, a couple of cigarettes, toilet paper, salt and pepper and the ever present Tabasco hot sauce. It is said that if you like

Tabasco sauce, you can make anything taste good. Well, I didn't like Tabasco sauce.

Well, to get back to my walk around Long Binh; I came across a find that was like a dream come true. I walked into their C-ration supply dump and there were cases and cases of C-rations. It must have been half of a good city block long with cases stacked thirty feet high. Well, I got talking to a couple of the guys working there, and lo and behold one was from Massachusetts! I can't remember where exactly, but he was a "homie," someone from my home state. I ended up with a whole case of C-rats, as we called them, and not just a small box, but a whole case. I could barely carry it back to the truck. Man that meant I could have my choice of meals anytime I wanted for probably the next month. I'd just bring it back to the hooch, put it in my locker and I'd be golden for a while.

I put the C-rats in the truck and soon the two other guys were back. It was then that I discovered we were not picking up anything, but dropping off instead. What we had brought up was the ever sought after, and rare in the Nam, air conditioner. The whole time I was there, the only time I felt air conditioning was the second day at MACV headquarters. The Senior Staff Sergeant advised me that he had arranged a swap with a buddy he had here at Long Binh; one air conditioner for a Jeep. That sounded good to me. We would get the Jeep later, that didn't sound good to me, but I had my C-rats, so I was happy. All we had to do now was get back to Saigon before dark, and it was already getting late.

Going back into Saigon, the traffic was tough. A young Vietnamese man on a motorbike was riding along beside us. He looked to be in his late teens and that would put him into the age of military service, but he wasn't in uniform, so that prompted some concern about what he was doing there and why he was so interested in us. I couldn't see a weapon and like I said he was on a motorbike. The gunner in back couldn't see him because it was a box truck with only the back open with no windows in the side. The Staff Sergeant next to me could only see a little of him as he was right up next to the truck on my side. It doesn't take much to hide a hand grenade and I was more than a little concerned. Then, another bike came up. This one was being driven by a male about the same age as the other. He passed number one and got in front of me. The traffic was getting heavier now and I knew that no matter what, I wasn't going to stop. They either wanted the truck to peddle on the black market, or to do harm to us and destroy the truck. We couldn't do anything because as it was, they had done nothing other than look out of place.

While I was contemplating what was going on, and what options I had as the driver, it kind of all came to a head. Bike number two in front of me started to turn right but there was no place for him to go because traffic was all backed up and stopped where he was going. He was about 30 feet in front of me and then he stopped. I think when he did that my heart stopped too. Number one was still beside me, about two feet behind my driver's side door (of course all the windows were down as it was about 100 degrees out). Well, most people are right handed and I figured if mope number one had a grenade that it would be tossed right handed and that would make it an off handed toss. But then again, that didn't mean a thing. I don't even know why I thought of that though, because by now, I was already cutting to the left instead of stopping. I clipped the number two bike right in the ass end. The driver stayed on his bike, but I pushed him around about 180 degrees and now he was kind of facing the truck. I shot by him and missed him and the rest of the bike by inches. Bike number one had to veer sharp left to keep from being turned into hamburg by the rear tires. I remember downshifting and trying to get the hell out of that situation. I got through it okay and kept going. To this day, I don't know what they had in mind, but I do know it was a setup. Nothing more ever came of it.

Chapter 14

When we got back at TSN, the guy in the back said, "Man I'm glad you didn't waste any time getting back." He never did know what went on up front; the lucky bastard. I got my case of C-rats to my hooch with no more problems. It was going to be good (well, for the time and place) eating for me for a while.

It was about this time I discovered a small bar on-base. It was right in back of our hooch next to some ARVN (Army Republic of Vietnam) barracks that were just a stone's throw from my hooch. It was nothing but a shack: no walls, just a roof with a bar. The whole thing couldn't have been more than twenty feet square, and the damndest thing, the bartender was no more than fourteen years old. There were no more than about twelve stools around the bar that covered three sides and the fourth side was a wall with a door way where, I guess, the kid lived and the beer was kept. There was a really good looking Vietnamese girl, probably 20 years old, there to get the G.I.s to stop in. I didn't know what her Vietnamese name was, but she said it translated into "Snow" in English. Beer was a buck a bottle and the kid, I don't know what his name was either, but if you didn't give him the buck, you didn't stand a chance in hell of getting a beer. It wasn't cold, but it was kept on ice in a cooler. They didn't always have American beer so at times, we drank the local beer that was called Ba Ba Ba. It was rumored that it was made with embalming fluid and from the taste one could believe it.

It was getting on into mid-November when I was called into the First Shirt's office for a meeting. I was told that I was going up country to hook up with the Third Marines. I had no idea if this was a good thing or bad. My heart was with the Corps, but I liked the thought of self-preservation too. I confided in the First Shirt that I felt I didn't know where I belonged, and I wanted to know what was going on. He leveled with me and said that I was part of an experiment; the Air Force did not have the training in the kind of combat that might occur in Vietnam. In WWII, the Air Force was part of the Army, but high security wasn't required at a base in England that was bombing Germany. In Korea, most bases were pretty secure and well protected. Here in the Nam, the bases were open to attack at any time and the feeling from MACV

89

was that something big was going on in the world of the Viet Cong. No one knew what, but all the top brass in Vietnam were aware that something was about to happen. As a result, the Air Force wanted people that had some military training, knowledge of how to handle a combat situation and had some insight into how to use troops in a combat situation. It was like he said, "Someone, somewhere, is covering their ass, and can say 'We have certain people that are trained in situations like this in case it happens so, we are prepared and can handle it.'" That was an interesting statement.

Now, I knew that it was just a test. I would go up country to where the real fighting was, learn some stuff and come back to my soft life. Looking at it that way, I guess I could handle it. But how was I supposed to get around and who would I report to? I was told I would fly to Da Nang and hook up with the Third Marines. My title would be Liaison Officer. I knew that in the Marines, it wasn't the rank that determined your position, or your job, but the requirement of the situation. So, that would fit okay. He said it would be no longer than a month and then I would be back. I didn't know if I could say no, but I said, "fine" and I went back to my hooch and started to put some things together.

Some of the guys wanted to know what was going on, and I just said I was going up North for a while. A couple of them said, "Now, wait a minute. That just doesn't happen like that." They mentioned how just a short time before; I had gone to Cu Chi. They wanted to know: what gives!? I ended up saying that I was checking on how to fight like soldiers and when I came back, I'd let them in on it. I packed light: some of my C-rats, my helmet, and my ditty bag with a toothbrush and the like. I'd learned that in the real world, all the essentials are pretty nonexistent in the world of survival. You carry what keeps you alive and comfort items that so many people say they can't live without are nothing but in your mind.

The next morning I was in a plane called a Caribou. It was a twin engine type with a funny bend in the wings and rear entry body. We landed a short time after takeoff, and I transferred to a C-123 aircraft. The C-123 was a larger; two engine aircraft that also loaded from the ramp in the rear. This one had liquid tanks inside. I talked to the crew chief before we took off, and he said that it was being set up to spray the new chemical they were calling "Agent Orange." It would kill all the vegetation that the Viet Cong hid in, and then we could go after them. I asked why it was called Agent Orange and he just answered, "Because it comes in big Orange drums." I could live with that. Then he asked me, "Know what our motto is?" "No," I answered back. He replied with a grin, "Only we can prevent forests." We both laughed. As the plane took off, it become too loud inside to talk.

As we flew north, I watched the mountains pass beneath us and thought that I was going to have to get a camera. The landscape was pretty, but it seemed everywhere I looked, I could see bomb craters. All of a sudden, the plane just started to drop, like we were falling out of the sky. I didn't have any idea what was happening and I yelled to the loadmaster over the noise of the engines. He had a flight helmet on that was hooked to the intercom of the airplane. I figured he might know what was going on. He came over to me and yelled in my ear that they were landing, and that was just how all the planes landed in the Nam; you drop fast to keep people from shooting at you. He also told me his unit designation was "The Ranch Hands" because when they were flying low to spray the Agent Orange, they were great targets, and it was a known fact that they were the most shot at unit in the service. I was sure glad they weren't spraying today. The landing was more like a controlled crash, and believe me the landing gear on the C-123 doesn't deploy very far down from the bottom of the plane, so I almost wanted to stand to save my ass literally from dragging on the runway, but it was all okay and stopped without any problem. Damn, I was feeling awful old when I got off that plane. I grabbed my ditty bag and started to look for the operations officer.

Chapter 15

Here I was again at a huge base, but this time, a Marine base. "Welcome to Da Nang," the officer said. He asked where my gear was and I said all I had was the one bag. He said he would fix me up with my 782 gear right away. I followed him to a supply hut and I was issued another rifle (I had turned mine in when I returned from Cu Chi). This time I was issued the M-14, and was told that I was with the Marines now and to get that silly ass Air Force shit off. Man, it sure was confusing at times. Anyhow, I was issued some very important gear, some of which included the Marine K-Bar knife, field mess kit, entrenching tool, poncho rain gear, field jacket with hood, among some other stuff. To this day I still have my helmet and K-bar knife. They mean everything to me even 40 years later.

I was told I was going to go out to Dong Ha combat base to 3rd Marine Division. There, I would be advised further on what I could do. I was to chopper out to a place called Phu Loc, then up to Camp Evans, then to Dong Ha. It would take a while and I would stay over at one of the bases en route, according to how the aircraft was flying. I felt lost, but was very happy I had thrown in some of my C-rats from my private stash into my ditty bag. All the choppers I flew in were the Huey 1Ds. They were a newer model than I had flown in when I was at Whiteman; at least I was comfortable being around them.

I learned I was classified as "Spare Parts" again, as I was being flown into the bases. Actually, they weren't really bases, but camps with the mail or anything else a camp might require as the bird was going by. The first night I stayed on a hilltop that was a new fire support base. This meant it had artillery on it to support the grunts in the field. I could never understand how they could hit a target a mile away or more with such accuracy. I had no idea then, but the artillery I couldn't understand would save my life one day.

These camps were small, and when I say small, I mean it. You could climb the observation post in the center of the camp and see the whole damn place. Barbwire was all around at least three rows deep. On the wire was a new tool of death for war use. It was called the Claymore Mine. It was an automatically detonated device about the size of a flattened out roll of paper towels colored gray and slightly curved. It could be detonated by a hand held clicker, by trip wire or any other way. It was very handy in war. When detonated, it fired out hundreds of steel ball bearing type projectiles in a concentrated direct fire to the front. I'll never forget the terrible, beautiful, peace of mind Claymores. And another thing I'll never forget; on each mine, printed on one side just as a footnote, you might see on a receipt very casual, except on the Claymore, it had printed "front toward enemy." It was just three words that had the intent and was a note that meant "to kill, face this way". This was a serious business I was in. I was learning to deal with death in a very impersonal way, and I was learning to ask the right questions, and believe me, you paid attention in this environment. It seemed impossible to me for anyone to penetrate the wire, claymores, and bunkers on the perimeter of the camp.

I would be sleeping in a bunker for the night; no comfy cot, just good old mother earth. This was a new camp and had no creature comforts, just the basic to keep people alive. Just before dark, myself and the five other grunts in the bunker had C-rats for chow. Whenever G.I.s had a chance to eat, the conversation after any formalities such as nicknames, home state or city and the such always seemed to turn to the date of, and the quality of chow we were eating. Some believed the cans of C-Rats were from World War II, but usually most believed they were from the Korean War. Everyone always had their own thoughts. There were no heater units or not-bad-tasting stuff the modern day warriors have today. Thinking back, no phones or computers and no thoughts of talking to anyone back in the world (that is what everyone called home) until your tour was over and you were out of the Nam. All those modern day inventions and are now called necessities were not even dreamed of in our time.

One of the grunts in the bunker relayed a story of when he was working with some Australian soldiers a while back (yes, the Australians were in the Nam with us, but had their own base of operations and usually did their own thing, which I heard were very good). Well anyway, this grunt had talked the Aussies into trying our issued C-rats instead of their own. Well, he had made a silent bet with another grunt that he could get the Aussies to dump the can of C-rats he was eating without even touching him. He said all he had to do is wolf his down before anyone had gotten halfway through theirs, casually turn his can over and say as if reading the bottom print on the can, "holy shit, it says 'not fit for human consumption'!!" and watch the Aussies turn their can over to read the bottom, thus dumping the contents out. I kind of doubted that it worked, but he says he won ten bucks on the bet. Well, it passed the time. I was learning that time was one thing we seem to have lots of. We, in turn, after chow made our trips to the latrine tubes and pits before dark. It seems to be the consensus that everyone should be squared away before dark, because night time was owned by the V.C.

One of the guys named Greenwood had the first watch with another grunt from the other bunker. There were only two observation posts. On the wire you could see two walls, well, see the strands of wire in two directions from each O.P. Fighting trenches were posted all along the inside of the wire. The cannon cockers, as they were called, slept in small dugouts next to their respective weapons. There were three cannons and a mortar section on this hilltop. The mortars could fire flares through the night at random times or when called to light up the area. The chug of the outgoing mortars lulled me to sleep.

I stirred a little when Greenwood came in from watch, and then dozed right off again. I must have been deep in sleep because at first, I thought I was dreaming when everyone was running like hell out of the bunker. Then, I heard an explosion, but it didn't seem to be very loud. I was already in my clothes, except for my boots. I got them on grabbed my flack vest, helmet, rifle and ammo and ran out of the bunker. Then it hit me, why am I going out of the bunker if we are under a mortar attack? Why not stay inside? Well, come to find out, a fighting trench is just about as safe as a bunker, thanks to good old mother earth, and the incoming rounds were aimed behind us trying to get the artillery not us. Seconded the mortars usually meant that a ground attack would be next. Everyone was looking for a flash or something that would indicate a firing point. The heavy weapons had their weapons registered in during the day for suspected problem spots at night and they had begun to fire on suspected areas just after the first incoming round had landed. I didn't see any more flares as the light could mess up any night vision scopes being used and might help the V.C. more than us. If there was a ground attack, that would change. The incoming stopped as fast as it started. It lasted about 10 minutes which seemed like an hour. Everyone was on guard now for the ground attack.

Chapter 16

The outgoing fire stopped shortly. It was around 3 a.m. or zero three hundred. Around zero five hundred, it started to get light and the threat diminished of any attack. No one was wounded on the line, but two guys from the artillery were; one from shrapnel in the arm and one lost two fingers when his hand was positioned wrong feeding cannon. The guys on the line were wondering later if the guy that lost his fingers would get a purple heart or not. A Purple Heart is a decoration issued to those wounded as a result of enemy action. The guy that had his arm messed up from shrapnel would. We just didn't know about a mistake you made during the rush of an attack. We would never know. A decision like that was up to the powers to be. As for me I believe in the saying I saw years later on a bumper sticker, "All gave some, some gave all."

As daylight came, life went back to normal. I was informed I would fly out after the medical "dust off" chopper took the wounded out; sometime before noon. Most of the guys checked the gear, policed up the area, checked the wire and claymores, and went back to the never ending job of filling sandbags for bunkers. As for me, I went up to talk to the mortar men. The mortar always interested me. It is a tube approximately 5 feet long or shorter depending on caliber, or as mortars go, millimeters such as the M29A1 81MM mortars I was shown. Most gunners take great pride in their weapons, and these mortar men fit right in. The tube stands up and the shell is hand dropped down the tube. An explosive charge at the base of the shell hits the firing pin at the bottom of the tube and sends it and the explosive head out of the tube up to three thousand yards or more. It can fire all kinds of shell including flares, high explosives, white phosphorus, and smoke. The 81MM is a large weapon. The 60MM mortar seemed less intimidating to me. A mortar is a close in defense weapon, whereas the artillery can reach out for miles and hit what they want. It all has to do with the trails and aiming stakes. You have to know what you are doing. With mortars, it is more about the angle of attack of the tube. A person on the outside of the service could never know how much depended on the youngsters in service doing the job right. So much depends on them. It doesn't matter if you are on a ship, flight line, or relaying a message by phone most of the time, there just isn't any room for a mistake. The job gets done and the training pays off, and someone down the line is better off for it. And back in the world there are people who won't let a sixteen year old mow the lawn because it is too dangerous. Sometimes you just have to shake your head.

On my way back to the CP, I filled up my canteens at the water buffalo and waited. The Medevac chopper came and went. It wasn't long before I heard another chopper coming. It turned out to be my ride. This one was a Chinook CH-46 chopper. It brought in more troops, ammo, supplies, and other miscellaneous stuff. I helped unload, gathered my gear and went aboard. This was one of the big twin rotor choppers. It loaded from a ramp that lowered in the back. It was always left down as far as I could tell. This chopper had a 50 Cal Machinegun up front. That sure is a lot of firepower compared to the M-60s the Huey has. It shows the power the Chinook had to lug all that weight and a full load. Helicopters sure are loud though. There is just no way to sneak up on someone in a chopper.

We were in the air for some time, and when we put down and were on the ground, I was talking to the crew chief and asked why this chopper, for such a large one, had only one set of landing gear in the front. All the large choppers I saw always had two sets for a total of four; one set on each corner. I was told that the Marines fly the CH46 chopper and the Army flies the CH47 bird. The difference mainly is the single front landing gear. Well, live and learn.

After shooting the shit and deplaning, low and behold, here I was back in DaNang. First thought: Oh, oh I'm screwed up. I found the operations officer and he told me to wait. So, I waited. After a long wait, an officer from personnel came by and picked me up. He told me that I would be going on an operation out towards the Annamite Mountain range. I stupidly asked, "Where is that?" He just looked at me and said, "Sergeant, you are going where you are told to go." And I said, "yes sir." I later learned that the Annamite Mountain range ran basically down the Western part of the Country and at times the mountains turned East and ran almost to the coast, the V.C. always used the mountains as protection for their field of operations, and it was always a hotly contested area of operations. After a short ride I was dropped off and introduced to a Staff Sergeant named Rand and was informed I would be going with his squad into the bush in the a.m.. I was told due to the fact that I was "spare parts," I could carry an extra " radio." I had no idea what he was talking about, but with the heat as it was, I knew I didn't want to carry any more weight than I had to. I just said, "Yes sir."

I was shown to a tent and set down on a box. There were a couple of guys in the place and we started to talk. After introductions and home states, and sharing that I was going out with them in the a.m., I got around to saying I would be carrying the extra radio. That is when a guy said, "Man you're going to carry another Prick-25." I didn't like the sounds of that, so I said hey, why not fill me in on this choice assignment? He said it was just a radio, but a heavy son of a bitch and with it goes a big target tied to your ass. I suddenly didn't feel too good after that. We had chow, and after chow, I met the rest of the guys. Four of the guys were on shit burning detail. That meant that they had to pull the drums that the troops use for bathrooms and burn the waste. It was required for sanitation reasons. There are always bad details in the service. Man, I thought cleaning the "head" (bathrooms) back at

Whiteman A.F.B. was bad. Well, it was too late to wake up and smell the roses now.

The mobile field kitchen we ate out of or around was O.K. but dipping your mess kit into that boiling water was always attention getting. I remember in training we were told if we drop anything into the hot water not to reach for it, for if you do you will lose your hand. A message like that sticks. After we got back to the tent we were told to leave our mess kits behind in the a.m.and we would move out in trucks at 06:00. Roll call 05:00. Soon after the guys settled down and had written their letters and got squared away, conversation turned to the new weapon the troops were being issued called the M-16. I turned to the focal point when I said that I had already qualified on the M-16. Some Marine units had already been issued the gun, and from all reports back, showed that it was terrible. They all had heard how that once in the field, it had to be kept spotlessly clean or the damn thing jammed. A gun that doesn't work when you need it means death to the owner. I had to add that the only time I had used mine was during the ride into Cu Chi, but that was only about 10 minutes, and was a clean gun that worked okay, but I sure didn't like what I heard, but this trip out we all had the M-14. No one slept very well that night and by 05:00, everyone was up and set for a briefing. Among other things we were told it would be about a three hour truck ride to our area of operations.

Chapter 17

Intelligence said that the North Vietnamese were more active on the Ho Chi Minh Trail along the border just inside the neighboring countries of Laos and Cambodia, sending all kinds of war materials and men south into South Vietnam with what seemed to be a build-up toward Da Nang. We were going to be part of a search and destroy deployment from Da Nang west towards the Laos border. We would be resupplied as needed by air. We were told to bring poncho liners as it would be colder in the higher elevations, something I wasn't expecting. The operation had no name, so simply it would be called the operation with "No Name."

After the briefing and chow we were given truck numbers to form up on. After chow, I asked the company C.O. why I had a radio. He said I was listed as spare parts as a Liaison officer, and all Liaison people knew how to work the radios. Surprise, surprise. I didn't. He said that is how they got the extra radio, and it was now my baby, and I was not to let anything happen to it. Just great! While we were waiting to saddle up, I caught up with the company RTO (radio transmission officer) for some pointers on the thing. He said I shouldn't have to use it and that the Company had all the frequencies to use. So basically, he showed me the on/off, the volume, and the dial for frequencies. I was told to leave it off so the batteries would be fresh. I then took my place in the back of a truck in an endless line of trucks. Everyone was carrying extra belt ammo for the machineguns we had with us, but because of the radio, I didn't have to. So in the end, everyone was overloaded in weight when we departed outside of Da Nang.

The rice paddies weren't as common I thought they would be as we traveled west. Two tanks traveled with us, mixed in with the trucks. Conversation revealed that the grunts had mixed feelings about the tanks. Their firepower and mobility on hard flat country was comforting, but the noise was a drawback. They had been known to run over a G.I. and not even know it. We were dropped off after about three hours, on schedule. We saddled up for the march into what seemed to be higher ground. Two squads were assigned tank protection. It seems the tanks can't work without the grunts in front to cover them from booby traps, or the one or two man tank killer teams with what is known as RPGs (rocket propelled grenades). So, as usual, the grunt is out in front.

Because I had a radio, I was to stay close to the CO, but not too close as he already had his own RTO with him. Thank you, Lord for the radio on my back. It was hot, muggy, and the grass plain we were in was awful. The grass could cut you if you weren't careful, and it was about four feet high so you couldn't see anything that was in it. I was sweating so bad; I wished I had put a towel on my neck like some of the other guys. There wasn't any chatter. Everyone was in their own thoughts, wishing they were somewhere else.

As we walked toward a tree line, the tanks stopped to scan the area with the strong gun sights they had. Everything seemed okay. As we continued to walk forward, I was just right of center, back about 15 feet from the front. I guess the line had fifty guys in it with about ten to twenty feet between them in a rough straight line. All of a sudden, all hell broke loose from the tree line and looking back, it seems you always draw fire from a tree line and higher elevation. Everyone went flat on their stomachs. There was someone yelling for a Corpsman on my left, so people were getting hit already. I couldn't see shit lying in the tall grass, and if you stood up, you were a target. I crawled up beside the grunt in front of me so I was on line and could fire to the front where it was very clear that only the enemy was to our front. Everyone was firing but no one could see a target.

The drill in this war, when you were drawing fire as we were, was to get close to the enemy before he could get into your range and hit you with mortars. So, we started crawling forward. I didn't feel scared at the time, just committed to doing the right thing and what was expected of me. I really believe no Marine is going to let another Marine down. We knew what was expected of us, and we were going to do it. In the middle of crawling forward in that grass, I could hear mortar shells landing all around us. I then heard someone say that we should have our bayonets on our rifles because in this tall grass, we could crawl right into someone and not know it until it was too late to aim and shoot. In the middle of all this chaos, for some reason, I remembered back in basic bayonet introduction the D.I. saying that if you bayonet the enemy and the bayonet gets stuck in a bone and you can't pull it out, just to fire your weapon and the recoil will dislodge it. The joke was that in every recruit training class, there was a guy in the

111

back that says with all the respect in his heart, "Sir, if I have any bullets in my rifle, there isn't no way I'm going to be close enough to bayonet someone." A person sure thinks of the damndest things at the damndest times, and that thought was only a fraction of a second. It was all business. I didn't have a bayonet so I was out of luck, but I prayed that if I got out of this alive, I'd never be caught without one again.

The M-14 is a powerful rifle and we were putting a lot of rounds out to the front, but no one could tell if it was any good or not. We were crawling to about 50 feet in front of the tree line by now and were told to hold in place: to just stop and continue to fire. We couldn't dig because if you moved around you attracted attention and drew fire. The M-60 machine guns were set up to the left and right of us. They were called "pigs" because they used a lot of ammo in a hurry, and the call for more ammo for the "pigs" was going up and down the line. When I say, "pigs," it can't be taken in a bad way, because those machine-gunners sure helped save the day, and they drew a lot of fire. I wouldn't want to be a gunner on one of those things.

Everyone was slowing down on the rate of fire because no one wanted to use up their ammo. All of this happened in about ten or fifteen minutes, if that. It sure seemed longer. In no time at all there were helicopter gunships raising hell with the tree line. Rockets and machine gun rounds were hitting everything in front of us. I heard a lot more than I saw because a lot of the time my face was buried into the dirt that I wanted to become a part of. Things started to quiet down pretty fast and as soon as the choppers let up, we moved right into the trees.

The smell of powder and burnt flesh was everywhere. I stayed right in line as we moved up. There were no more mortars or small arm fire like before, but we moved like in slow motion and with great care. The trees and bushes that had such big leaves were all gone. Everything was chewed to hell. We came across some fighting holes the V.C. were in. Some had some body parts in them, but we didn't find any wounded or whole bodies. That is when my time at Cu Chi clicked in. There had to be tunnels in the area. That many people don't just disappear.

Some of the guys started looking around and checking for booby traps and the like. Others checked for papers or anything else that could hold important information as to the enemy's plans, strengths or weapons. It was pointed out in short order that by the looks of some of the uniforms on the body parts that were left behind that we were not engaged with a common Viet Cong unit, but what was called "Mr. Charles," or a unit of the North Vietnamese Army. The uniforms told the difference. The V.C. always seems to wear black, pajama-type clothes with flip flop type sandals. From what we could see, these people had uniforms on with different foot gear. Their fighting positions were planned and well dug, almost like dealing with a professional compared to a fly-by-night operator.

Some patrols were sent out to check the area and see if we were secure or not. We were told to dig in for the night. There were a lot of mixed feelings: whether to use the holes dug by the former real estate owners or go for a little higher ground and dig our own holes. The argument being that if we used a hole already dug, the former occupants would know exactly where you were if he attacked during the night. The upside was that all the work had already been done for us and we just had to move in and occupy the holes. Well, smart thinking won out and we moved to a new location and dug in. We dug and ate our C-rats and dug some more. Two man holes, one man awake at all times. Trip flares were set out, claymore mines set, artillery from a fire base was zeroed in around us, more ammo was issued, and we settled in for the night. We could do two hour watches or four hour watches. It didn't matter to me because I knew I wasn't going to sleep anyway.

Chapter 18

I was paired up with a marine named Azar Mathews from a place called Washburn, Colorado. He was a Private and I was the Sergeant. I chose the four hour watch, thinking that it was better to get a chance to sleep a little longer than having to be awakened every two hours. Who could sleep? I'll tell you, when you share a foxhole with a guy, you become closer than you could believe. We talked in a whisper back and forth about everything.

Azar had been in country about six months, and this was his second time in the bush. He said the first time was in what was called operation Union 2 in May, right after he got in country. His feelings seemed to be that the V.C. owned the country and we just kept prodding him here and there. He said that Union 2 was further south of where we were now, and that today showed that Union 2 hadn't changed a thing. We show up and the V.C. are there waiting for us. We have a fight and lose some people, and kill some of them, and then they disappear. We say we won and move on, so we can do it all over again: fight, get some people killed, kill some of them, and then they disappear. We move on, say we won, then three months later, come back to the same spot and do it all over again and say we won. It just didn't make any sense. It kind of makes you wonder. Well, we had a task at hand, and that was to stay alive and do our job. I told Azar that I really liked his name and if I ever got married and had kids, my first boy's name would be Azar. He sure got a chuckle out of that. I guess no one likes their own name.

By now, it was getting dark, so no more talking and no smoking for the guys that did. We laid some grenades out within reach for a fast throw if need be. There were no overhanging trees close to us, so we knew we could throw a grenade, rather than having to toss it underhand to avoid branches that would hang it up and possibly drop it back onto you. Little things like that can mean a lot and to stay alive, you notice everything around you.

The foxholes next to me and Azar were about ten feet on either side. Ten feet isn't much, but during a night when it is pitch black, it sure seems a long way. A person can crawl within five feet of you and drop a grenade in your hole before you know anything is wrong. Number one rule: don't do anything that gives away your position. No noise. Don't even breathe too loud.

Azar had the first watch. He was to wake me if I was still sleeping at midnight. The hole we dug wasn't very big, probably three feet deep by four or five feet long. I hunkered down, sitting in the dirt with my feet across his legs as he kneeled to keep an eye over the edge. It wasn't comfortable, but before I knew it, the adrenaline rush of the fight earlier had just drained me and I was out. I must have been out an hour at the most when I woke with a start. I was cold and scared. Azar was okay. I couldn't get back to sleep, so I joined Azar, staring into the night. We didn't talk for fear of giving our position away. It sure was a black night. We knew the grunts next to us were there, but we couldn't see or hear them, just like they knew we were here, but they couldn't see or hear us. Just 10 feet separated us. It could have been 10 miles.

After a while, Azar pointed to his watch, showing it was midnight. It was now my turn on watch. He laid down and man did I feel all alone. I couldn't see anything, and sometimes I would close my eyes so I could hear anything different.

Nothing--just the night sounds. The hairs still stand up on the back of my neck when I think of that night. I was so tense that I ached all over. I glanced at my watch and it was only 12:30. I couldn't believe it. I would have sworn it had been two hours. Time just dragged. At times I was sure I detected a movement out front, but only a bush or leaf could stay that still for that long.

The next glance at my watch showed 03:30. Just 30 more minutes and I could wake Azar and take a break. I was just going to nudge Azar awake when I heard a thud, then an explosion. Azar was up in an instant. There were more thuds and more explosions. We looked at each other, knowing that the thuds we had heard had to be the mortar firing. That meant that they were close, very close. We looked for a muzzle flash and thought we could see something out front a short ways. The explosions were behind us so they were off on their range. We had done a great job of keeping our positions hidden. In the flash of the explosions, I could see the guys in the hole next to ours on our right pointing where we were looking. Good training pays off. But now what? If we fired, we would give away our position and bring the fire on us. What we would have given for a grenade launcher. We couldn't throw a grenade that far.

Without any hesitation, Azar grabbed the three grenades we had and said, "I'm going next door. I'll be right back." With that, he crawled out of the hole and slithered into the hole on our right. He was back in a flash with two more grenades. He gave me one and said he was going to get the mortar. The two guys from the other hole were to crawl out of their hole about 50 feet. I was going to go out the same distance on the left and Azar, right up the middle with the grenades. If his plan didn't work and he was spotted, we would have the V.C. in a crossfire in front of us when he pulled back. Then we would all split to our respective holes.

About 5 minutes had passed since the first shell had landed and we started out. It was calm to our front; now all we had to worry about was friendly fire coming down on us. We crawled as fast as we could on line, then Azar went ahead. We hadn't thought that the mortar might have rifle cover. Azar was about 25 feet in front of us when he tossed the first grenade with two more right after. The mortar went silent, then rifle fire started coming and I could hear the crack of bullets all over the place. Azar was back with us and we started spraying the whole area to our front as we backed up on our guts to our holes. I didn't realize until we had dived into our foxhole that there were shells still coming into our lines. That meant we had knocked out one mortar. There had to be a couple more somewhere.

Chapter 19

Now small arms fire was breaking out all over. The two tanks that were with us were behind us. They don't do too much in the close confines of the trees. They were firing their 50 Cal over us to the front, and things were getting very loud. Flares were coming from somewhere. Maybe from the tanks? But we didn't see any people to our front; just muzzle flashes, so we fired at the flashes. The same as they were doing to our flashes.

After a short time, we started to see the N.V.A. coming out of the trees, a lot of them. Now we had something to aim at. In retrospect, this was my moment of truth. I was going to kill a human being. I didn't feel any emotion or thought at that time. People were trying to kill me and I had to stop them. Like all of us, I aimed and fired. Now the tanks got into the act with huge explosions in the line coming at us. People would disappear in an explosion but more just kept on coming. I tossed the last grenade and kept shooting. There were more explosions to our front then the tanks could ever put out, and we knew it was artillery from one of our fire bases. With all that firepower, the N.V.A. just started to melt away.

It wasn't until the firing really died down that I realized that it was getting light out. Everyone stayed down, because the artillery was still coming in, but had shifted further away as if chasing people back through the jungle. At about 06:45, guys were starting to stand up in their holes and talk. I told Azar that I thought it was incredible how he took over and knocked out the mortar. He was the bravest person I'd met. Someone said that a hero is a person who "does what has to be done when it has to be done, no matter what the consequences." He was a hero in my book. He just said, "Hey, you guys were with me."

Everyone started to get into the routine. Some cleaned their rifle, others took inventory of what was needed, and others started eating C-rats. Being an N.C.O., I walked up to the Command area to listen and see: what now? I'd been on the ground for less than 24 hours and couldn't even think straight. Looking at the Lieutenant and Captain, I couldn't believe how haggard they looked. Up until now, all the officers I'd seen were clean and sharp. These guys looked dirty, drawn and worn out. The Staff Sergeant, who told me to carry the radio, asked who I was. He didn't recognize me. I told him and he asked where the radio was. I told him it was okay in my hole. He said go get it and turn it over to Humble, who is assigned to Headquarters Co. So I went back to my foxhole, retrieved the radio and started looking for Corporal Humble. He was up with the Captain. He took it like he wanted it. A load off my back. The Captain told me to go back to my area and tell the guys that we were shoving off in about an hour. I went back, but the guys already knew we were going out, so I ate, cleaned my rifle and gathered my thoughts.

The C-rations didn't seem so bad after all. In fact, from the case that was brought up to us, I drew a breakfast issue of eggs and ham, and I was kind of fond of them. They weren't real eggs (I don't think), and the ham was spam. You know what the Grunts say about Spam: it is a ham that didn't pass its physical. In any case, I kind of liked it. As a youngster in a poor family we ate a lot of spam, my mother would mix water with brown sugar and serve it over spam and mashed potatoes, it was a real treat.

Choppers came in and brought in another company and took out the poncho covered bodies of the guys killed in the fight. The wounded were airlifted out at first light. The rumor mill was going full strength. The new company was told that we were engaged with a full strength North Vietnam Army Battalion. That meant we were out numbered about three to one, but we had much superior fire power, and we hadn't hit the main body yet. It seemed that the V.C. sure had a lot of people on their side. We were told that we would advance to a little rise about a 4 hours' march from here and dig in. A recon squad was already out as point, and we followed shortly.

It was hot and humid, and we were walking up a constant grade in the jungle. The sun was out, but it seemed dark under the foliage of the jungle. We walked in mostly a single file now and slow. After about two hours, I heard some shooting up front and everyone stopped and got off the trail. We stayed stopped for a while and then started moving again. I became worried about my water supply as I had two canteens: one empty and the other about a quarter full. I always worried about having enough water to drink I'd recall my childhood growing up in the town of Sterling Ma. In the house we lived in my mother, father, older brother, and two sisters and me. We didn't have a well; all we had was a big wooden barrel that was in our 12 foot by 12 foot dirt floor cellar. A lead one inch pipe ran across our neighbor's yard and up a small hill to a spring on their property. My father had water rights to the spring and pipe. Water was clean and cold and I could remember going up into the woods on some nights holding a flashlight for my dad while he dug out some of the mud that would wash over the screen on the end of the pipe and stop the flow of water. Anyway the water would run just about all year, and when the barrel got full it would flow out of a small pipe at the top and into the ground of the cellar. We had an electric water pump to pump the water out of the barrel up to the bathroom and kitchen sink. There was no heat in the house other than the oil kitchen stove, so in the winter a blanket was hung in the kitchen doorway to keep the heat in and the cabinet doors on the sink were left open to keep the pipes from freezing. The main water problem would usually occur around the end of August if it was really dry, you see the spring would dry up, and that meant no water for the house. One time when I was about six years old we had no water, so when that happened we would go to our neighbors in the other direction, their names were

Link and Sylvia Wiggin, really nice people. They had a small pond on their property, that all the kids would swim in in the hot weather. Well we could haul pails of water to fill up our barrel from the pond. Well like I said I was about six and had a little red wagon, so I put two big buckets in the wagon went over to the pond and filled the buckets up, it was some load for the small wagon and a six year old, but I was doing a man's job and I felt great. I got the water back to my house and was pulling the wagon up onto the sidewalk to our backdoor to go down cellar, we didn't have a bulkhead it was just a trap door in our back room with some stairs. Well I pulled the wagon up to the walk and the whole thing tipped over and all the thoughts I had of doing good drained into the yard. It broke my heart for I had worked so hard to get that water home to my folks. Water always met a lot more to me after you don't have it, I never forgot that. We didn't get a well until I was sixteen. We hand dug the five foot deep trench the forty feet to the well pipe after the well was put in. I ended up working for the well driller for the summer, I sure learned a lot. His name was Herbie Russell , and in those days there were no rotary drills, just what was called ground pounders and it sure was some thrill working with them, climbing the derrick and setting the cables to run everything. It was rugged work in all kind of weather, but I loved it. So anyway I was thinking how I knew what it was like to be thirsty. And that sure isn't much water in humid, 100 degree heat, with a load on your back, walking up hill. We stopped one more time for a break of about 10 minutes and we were off again.

Chapter 20

At about noon, my line broke into a little clearing on a rise and the whole company was there. Some of the grunts had chainsaws and were cutting trees down, making a landing area for choppers, and at the same time, making a better field of fire down slope. It just amazed me as a combat soldier we were only aware of the 50 or so feet area that was directly around us, but that the powers to be had this area all planed out and were making it a suitable place to defend in an attack. Everyone was assigned a task. I was with two other N.C.O's. and we were in charge of digging fighting holes. We all dug together. Some guys were using C-4 explosive to blow stumps. C-4 is a soft explosive that can be shaped in any form, dropped or cut and it won't explode until set off with a cap. When it goes off, it is so powerful it travels at a speed of 5 miles a second -- great for landscaping. We talked the engineers into popping a couple of holes for us to save on some digging. It sure worked well.

The tanks were not with us anymore, but the reinforcements were well supplied. As soon as an area was cleared, choppers started bringing in more ammo, barbed wire, claymores, water and C-rats. Some more people came in also. Some of the old timers were saying that we were getting too much stuff, so something had to be up. The feeling was that we were being set up to draw the V.C. to us. That sure didn't make a person comfortable thinking about it. We worked cutting, clearing, and digging for the rest of the day.

As an N.C.O., I was privy to some of the information coming out of Headquarters Company. The N.C.O.s were told to know where all the fighting holes and trenches were in our area and to make sure everything was set to defend our area. There would be all the ammo, grenades and support we would need. We all had the feeling that we were the bait in a rat trap. Bring the NVA to us, and then hammer the hell out of them with our tremendous firepower. The problem that we all saw was that the bait was small enough to be eaten by the rat before the trap could kill him. That wasn't a good feeling.

We all filled sand bags to put around our holes to make them a bit higher and secure. We seemed to have everything we needed. The extra ammo was dished out, and we had people that had M-79 grenade launchers with us. A grenade launcher is a single shot, shoulder, fired like a rifle weapon that fires a round the size of a hand grenade out a great distance very accurately. The round is self-priming, so if it hits foliage or a tree in the first 80 feet or so, it won't go off. In the jungle, that is a very important factor.

Just before it started to get dark and I looked around, I was thinking that our little knoll looked like an ant hill. We had everything we required. The other thought was we had made enough noise all day long, so the bad guys sure knew where we were, and with that many people in such a confined area, if they started dropping mortars on us, there was no way a lot of people were not going to get hit. I started to dig my hole deeper.

There was a lot of Corpsman, or Docs as we called them, around. The landing area we made could take one Ch-46 chopper, or two Hueys. Choppers were coming and going all the time it seemed. Something big was up. Right around dusk, word was passed for everyone to keep their heads down as spotter rounds of friendly fire started coming in to zero in around our area. A person sure starts thinking at a time like this.

I was sitting in my hole, thinking about opening up a can of C-rats, when Corporal Humble dropped in. Come to find out, he was from Massachusetts, from a small town in the western end of the state. Being here in the Nam, so far from everywhere, anyone from your home state was like a neighbor to you. We talked about the state and it was comforting to dream of home. The spotter rounds came in, and that was comforting. Maybe things wouldn't be that bad after all. Humble, or Big "H" as he was called, asked if he could work it so he could share my foxhole for the night. We figured Azar could fill in his spot at H.Q. Company. Well, Azar thought that was great because HQ was behind the line, not on it. So Big H and the radio I had given him stayed in my foxhole.

We split up our C-rats and had a feast. Word was passed: full alert for the night. That meant no chatter, sleeping, smoking, or moving around. Well, it wasn't dark yet, so we tried to relax some, maybe even nod off for a while. I guess after being in service, a person learns that they sleep anywhere, at any time, if need be. There was kind of a trick that was common in the Nam. I don't know if it was carried forward from other wars or not, but we knew that in the limited space we had, you couldn't lay down. Instead, we would sit back to back, leaning against each other. It works and is comforting for some reason, and as miserable as we were, you knew you weren't alone and that your partner was in the same shape as you. Well, anyway it works.

Before we knew it, it was getting very dark, so we started peering over the top of the foxhole. We had it in our minds that if we were going to get hit, it wouldn't be until after midnight, most likely just before dawn. Time dragged, but why would anyone want to rush what was coming? I started to think of a strange habit I was picking up. I remember for some reason from the first time I used my rifle outside Cu Chi, then in the grass before the tree line, and the night we were attacked in the trees, for some reason, I had the habit of cocking my rifle when the shooting started. This was stupid. Myself, as well as everyone else has their weapon loaded with the safety on. When it's needed, a person just flicks the safety off and the weapon is ready to use. Well for some reason, I flick the safety off, but instead of firing, I cock the rifle which in turn ejects a live round and chambers another one, then I fire. For the life of me, I don't know why I did that. It was stupid. Not only did it waste time, it wasted a live round. I wanted to get rid of such a dumb bad habit.

Chapter 21

We waited and waited. It was like sitting in a dentist's chair before the shot of Novocain. You sure aren't looking forward to it, but you know it is coming. I don't know what time it started, probably around 3AM or 03:00. It wasn't like before -- no mortars or explosions. It started as a burst of fire from down the line and we heard yelling: "Gooks in the wire." We didn't see anything. Then there was some firing from the hole next to us and some small arms fire from the woods around us. Then it stopped and one of the guys next to us said that he had been hit. Big H crawled over to the hole to see what was going on. He came back and said one of the guys was sneaking a smoke in the hole, and the glow of the butt must have tipped off a sniper as to where the hole was. The guy standing watch, as he was supposed to, got shot. I didn't smoke then, and to this day I hate cigarettes and have a strong dislike of people that do. I feel that the butt that is so important to them, is more important than life, even someone else's if need be. What a terrible waste. Big H said that because he was the biggest guy, he was going to carry the guy back to the aid station and would be right back. I wonder how the guy that was smoking felt. I guess I can understand why Big H was taking him back. He left and a claymore mine went off to my front and I shot at something I saw move about 20 feet away.

There was no big attack, only Gooks in the wire out front. It was only 5 minutes and Big H jumped back in the hole and I asked him how it went. I heard a voice and a language I didn't know. It was Vietnamese. I was in trouble. I spun to my right and a V.C. was right there. He had a hand on the radio that Big H had left behind. I brought my rifle up, and then all went black. I woke up about, I don't know, maybe 30 seconds, maybe 5 minutes later. My face was all numb and I knew I was bleeding from my mouth. The V.C. was still there, but wasn't moving. It seemed that when I brought my rifle up, he hit me in the mouth with his rifle but when he did, I must have squeezed the trigger because he had one hole right in the chest. I remember I couldn't talk and was very sick. I had to keep my head down as blood was flowing out of my mouth. My tongue told me that where my front teeth were was all busted up. I shot the V.C again to make sure he was dead than collapsed. I can't remember a thing that was going on around me. I thought of Captain Schmidt at Whiteman Air Force Base: the man who gave me my life back. He was a dentist and worked so hard on fixing my teeth when I was there. He was a great guy. Now all of that work was gone.

Laying there with the dead V.C. soldier, I thought I was bleeding to death. I couldn't talk or move. All I could do was sit half way up and keep my head tilted forward so I wouldn't choke to death on my own blood. I wondered why the North Vietnamese soldier hadn't just shot me when he could have. It just didn't make any sense to me. He could have just wasted me by shooting into my hole. Then I remembered the radio. He was after the radio. He had his hand on it when I turned around. The radio saved my life in a way, but in another, it was why he came to my hole in the first place. They must have been watching us all day and knew there was a radio in my foxhole. That was what they wanted. They must have seen Big H leave the hole and then made their move. They knew that if they shot into the hole, they might destroy the radio, and they had to have it working. Any more than one man might attract attention, or if there was more than one, the claymore that went off got them. So it was my luck that I had only one visitor.

I don't know how long it was, but I knew I was drifting in and out of consciousness and dreaming of never being alone again, even with the world exploding around me. I was just giving up when I felt something hit my leg and I heard someone yell, "Stoddard is dead." It just couldn't be. I couldn't speak so I moved my arm. It was Big H. "Jesus," he said. He thought I had had it. In the dark, and with the blood and my mouth was open like it was, he thought my face was gone from the nose down. He grabbed me and pulled me out of the hole. He grabbed the radio, but with his rifle and gear and tired from one run to the aid station already, he couldn't manage it. He threw the radio back into the hole with the dead V.C., pulled the pin on a grenade and threw it in. He yelled "grenade," to keep everyone's head down and blew everything in the hole to hell. So much for the praised "Prick-25." It either saved my life or almost took it. But how I love Marines. They can make a decision when it needs to be made, and they stick together.

Big H half carried, half dragged me to the aid station. I believe that if it was an officer that had found me, the radio might have been more important than a wounded Marine, and I would have had to lay there until a stretcher was sent out for me.

Thank you Big H, where ever you are. May God bless you.

Chapter 22

At the aid station I completely collapsed. I woke up on a chopper and knew I was enroute to a hospital. I had my helmet and wouldn't let go of it for some reason. I don't know how long the flight was, but it wasn't long. I was told as I was taken off the chopper and that I was at 1st Medical Battalion Da Nang. I was brought into a room where my bandages were taken off and then transferred to another room. When I woke up, it was dark. I was on a cot in the hospital with a hundred other guys. I didn't feel anything, but didn't want to. I just laid there and didn't move. Just like thousands of guys before me, you just lay there, not knowing what was going on or how you got there. I don't know if it was a day or a week, but an orderly (or maybe it was a doctor) came by to talk to me. He said all my front teeth were gone, so they operated and cleaned me up. He said that it wasn't as bad as it seemed and they were going to fix me up like new. I didn't need the pep talk. After looking around at the guys I was with, I knew I was lucky. I almost felt ashamed I was there.

Only three days after I woke, I was out. I was told I would be on light duty and could go back to my unit. I went to personnel to find out how to get back into the field and was told I was to fly back to Tan Son Nhut. I told them I would rather stay with the company and wanted to know what had happened, but that was not to be. I would fly south that day so I was to stand by until a plane was headed that way -- spare parts again. Seeing that I had to wait for I didn't know how long, I decided to write a sentiment on my helmet, one that I had seen on someone's flack vest, and I felt it was true about Vietnam. So with pen in hand, I wrote on my helmet cover: "If I had a home in hell, and a ranch in Vietnam, I'd sell my ranch and go home." This I printed on the side of my helmet and it was the start of a rough diary of dates, names and places I was to go. I also printed my full name, serial number and blood type (AB positive) on the side of my helmet.

Well, after a bit, I was called to "saddle up," and hop onto a plane headed south. When I landed at TSN, I went directly to the first Sergeant. He said he was sorry I was injured and that he would see to it that I was taken care of. It struck me funny that he used the word "injured" and not wounded. I was back in the 377th Combat

141

Support Group. I went back to my hooch, picked out a clean uniform, cleaned up some more and then laid down on my rack. It was daylight when I woke up, but I didn't have a clue as to what day it was. It could have been the same day or the next day. I just didn't know. It really had to be the next day, because I got up and went directly to the hospital at TSN. I explained my situation and they said they would get my records from 1st Bat. and go from there. I went back to my routine in the inspection section. I visited the little bar by my hooch, went down to the U.S.O. club in Saigon, and started enjoying life. I wanted to go back up north to see the guys I fought and almost got killed with, but I was a coward. I don't know what I would do if I learned Azar or even Big H had been killed. I just stayed in my own world on easy street.

A couple of days after I got back to my duty station, the Sergeant that I drove to Long Binh in the truck with looked me up and said he had picked up the jeep that was promised to him for the air conditioners. He told me that I could use it to go to chow from my duty station as it was such a long walk every day. My guess was that it was two miles each way, so that would put me on Easy Street when the jeep was available. I got a chance

142

to check it out, and it was a standard, what we called, MUTT. It was complete with canvas top and the required metal cable cutter welded to the front bumper. The cable cutter was a piece of iron that stuck up in the air about five feet and welded to the bumper so if any wires or the such were strung across a roadway you were traveling on, it would cut the wire before it took your head off. It sure was great to have a jeep to drive around, and because I was one of the few troops that had the correct license to drive, I was all set. The thought did enter my mind that I might be driving a stolen jeep, but I still enjoyed it.

Christmas was coming and I learned that the comedian Martha Raye was coming to the base to put a show on, so one night, I found myself, along with about three hundred other G.I.s, watching the great Martha Raye. She performed on the back of a flat trailer bed and did a show called "Hello Dolly." She had a whole troop with her. It was going fine when about half way through, the generator for her electrical system died. It wouldn't start, so she walked out on the truck bed/stage, set down on the side and just talked to us. It still brings tears to my eyes to think how somebody as famous as she was acted so happy to see us, when we were the ones so happy to see her.

She was a great person. I'll never forget the kindness of that lady.

Christmas was coming. The new base exchange was built and they were building two story barracks at the base. It was becoming a base, just like stateside. I just couldn't figure it out: didn't the brass know there was a war going on? The new Base Exchange at Tan Son Nhut was just like a Wal-Mart here in the states, but for some reason I preferred the military exchange located in the Cholon section of Saigon. A bus ran there and back from the U.S.O. building. It was always packed, like everything else in the service, but you could get your toiletries and trinkets and the like to send home for Christmas. Cholon, I was told, was the Chinese section of Saigon, and a little richer than downtown. Even downtown Saigon was packed with Americans, from civilian employees to G.I.s from every branch of the service, mixed in with the Korean soldiers that were there helping us fight as well as the Thailand soldiers and the Australians. Now, add fifty thousand Vietnamese to that and you can get the picture. A person could buy anything on the open black market in the shops in Saigon center. A lot of the officers in the Air Force and other branches stayed in downtown Saigon in hotels that had been rented by the U.S.

Government for officer's barracks or B.O.Q.s as they were called.

Chapter 23

Christmas came and went, and the American New Year's came and went. I say the "American" New Year's because in Vietnam, they celebrate the New Year holiday on the last day of January, not the first, as we do. To show how political the war was, during the holidays, the North Vietnamese with the South Vietnamese and United States, agreed on a cease fire over the holidays so we did not take any action in anyway against the North. All bombing stopped. Everything stopped. Well, all our operations against the V.C and North Vietnamese Army stopped, but all it did was give the V.C and North Vietnamese army the opportunity to regroup, restock and plan new attacks. As for us in the field, we couldn't understand how we could be killing each other and then a politician could say, "Okay, it is a holiday, so we won't kill you anymore until after the holiday is over." If they can stop for a holiday, why can't they stop forever?

I remember Christmas Eve in our hooch. There was about seven of us sitting around, drinking beer and at about 21:00 hours (9 p.m.), we started singing Christmas carols. It was kind of sad, and we couldn't sing a damn, but it seemed like home . It lasted about 2 hours. I don't remember anything about New Year's. It was just... Happy New Year! It was going to be 1968; the year we returned to the world. It had to be a good year. About the second week of January, the government fitted me with new front teeth. It was something new. They were permanent and I looked normal once again. That sure meant a lot to me.

Some of the guys in the hooch were living in Saigon with their Vietnamese girlfriends. This sure was a strange place. As for me, I didn't want anything to do with them. I once asked the girl at the bar I went to what she would do if the Americans left. In general, I meant what the Vietnamese people would do when the Americans left. She knew what I meant, and I'll never forget her answer: "No sweat," she responded. "Someone else will come. After all, the French were here before you." I was thinking, they must think this is a game or something. It just wasn't right. Nothing seemed right.

A couple of days after the first of January, a guy named Sameck was drunk in the barracks and started boasting to anyone there, probably three or four guys he was drinking with, that I was an undercover cop, spying on the guys in the hooch to see if they had any drugs or such. I have no idea what brought it on, other than no one knew what I did. Well, one thing led to another and we ended up in a fight. I was so afraid of getting hit in the mouth. I just went ballistic on him. I was going to put him down so he could never threaten or intimidate me ever again. It took all the other guys there to pull me off of him, but mission accomplished. No one was ever going to screw with me ever again. They knew it and I knew it.

Well, I guess I thumped him pretty bad, because a couple of days later, we were all called into the first Sergeant's office. It was a small office in a row of buildings at T.S.N. Everyone in the hooch was required to be there. I was a little nervous, but it was a known fact that Samek was drunk and pushing me. The other guys weren't hostile to me in anyway, in fact, the consensus was that Samek had been asking for it and just picked the wrong guy to mess with. It wasn't really a fair fight, for he was pretty drunk, but he also was an asshole even when he was sober. The first shirt listened and then spoke. I was kind of embarrassed by what he said. He said that he knew me, and he knew what kind of soldier I was, and that I wouldn't be shit on by anyone. That I was honest and knew what I was doing. He ended by making me Barracks commander over everyone else. Hell, I didn't want the job, but I just stood there. We all walked out of the office together and they all agreed they had been out of line, but they were really surprised how the first shirt stood up for me. I was too. We all went back to the hooch.

After a couple of days, I called a meeting one night. I told the guys that I didn't picture myself as a leader and I didn't want the position as Barracks C.O. I wasn't comfortable with it. Now, there was one guy in the hooch from Pottstown or Pottsville, Pennsylvania. I don't remember his name, but everyone liked him and he was what you would call a born leader. He just had a way about himself that people liked. I asked if it was okay with him and everyone else that he would be the barracks commander. He said yes, and everyone agreed, so we just let it be. Everything was fine.

Chapter 24

The next day, I was going up to the new Base Exchange to finally get the camera I had been thinking about and I noticed a guy in Air Force Fatigues get out of a deuce and a half where he had been manning an M-60 machine gun. The truck was an Army Big Red One outfit so I asked him what gives. He said he was with the same combat support group I was, but was assigned to the Big Red One engineer unit for combat experience. Boy did that ring a bell. Well, we hit it off right away. His name was Wagner, and we became friends. Man he was crazy, but in a fun way. We started to hang around together, as we were the only two people in our unit that did what we did. He tended to drink a little more than me, and that was hard to do as I was drinking a lot so I could sleep at night. I remember he stole an army TT unit (tractor trailer). You see, military vehicles don't have keys, so they are always ready to go. So, if the rightful owner doesn't chain the steering wheel, anyone can jump in and go. That is exactly what Wagner did one night. There was one problem though; he couldn't drive the damn thing, and the trailer took out a security guard shack on the road to our company area. I don't know how he got out of that mess, but he did somehow. Well, hanging around with Wagner was something to do.

One day we went to the BEMO and got Air Force survival knives issued to us. They were smaller than the K-Bar knife I had from the Marines, but the Air Force knife had a stone that you could use to sharpen the blade built right into the knife case. I liked that feature, so I put it on my web belt with my canteen and medical kit and put my K-Bar in my locker. Everything was pretty normal for about a month, and then January 30th, 1968 came. The Vietnamese were really excited about their lunar new year. Me? I just went to bed as usual.

I guess it was about five in the morning of the 31 st when I was awakened by an airman I knew from my section. His name was Ed Darden and he was pulling Charge of quarters duties. Charge of quarters was assigned to squadron personnel on a rotating schedule. It was the duty of the C.Q. to answer the squadron phone and to act as a fire watch around the hooches when we were sleeping. I remember him waking me very calmly and saying that the V.C. were taking Saigon and were very close. At first, what he was saying didn't register, and he was so calm, it didn't make any sense at all. I cleared the cobwebs out of my head and he repeated that the V.C. were taking Saigon and were really close. I then noticed that he had a helmet on which was very unusual for him. I didn't ask him why he woke me up, because everyone else seemed to be sleeping, but I got right up. He now had my undivided attention. I could hear small arms fire not very far away. I thanked him and he disappeared. I have no idea where he went.

I got dressed, and now, the small arms fire was a lot closer. Some of the other guys in the hooch were beginning to stir. I went out our door to the rear and went up to the first hooch I was in, as that one was right on the perimeter of the base on the Saigon City side. By now, I was crawling on my stomach and could hear a lot, and I mean a lot, of small arms fire right across the road and field that separated the base from the city. The road was hot top with a sidewalk about 50 feet from me, and as I live and breathe, walking up the sidewalk come two airmen. Now, you could hear the gunfire and see some flashes, and these guys are just talking and walking along as if they are in down town U.S.A.! I couldn't believe it. They were about even with me as I lay there in the dirt next to the hooch. No one else was around. I heard someone yell, "halt!" and they just kept on walking and talking. Then I heard a very strained voice yell "HALT!" It was very high pitched, as if someone was close to panic. The two guys stopped and a base security police officer, as the Air Force called its Military Police, pulled the two mopes into the ditch next to the road.

Most of the guys were up now, but didn't have a clue as to what was happening. No one had a weapon or even thought they might need one. I crawled back to my hooch and tried to figure out what was going on. I mean, I went to bed about 6 hours ago and everything was normal. Now, it seems everyone here is in trouble. I remember being told that the brass thought something big was going to happen. I wondered if this was it. If it is, what am I to do? The C.Q. Darden didn't say anything. I thought he woke me because he knew me and wanted to clue me in. He didn't say anything else. He just disappeared. If he had any orders for me, I'm sure he would have told me. He was the type of guy that you could depend on, and I thank him now if I didn't thank him then for giving me a "heads up."

In my hooch, along with the others, it seemed the guys were getting up to go to work just as if nothing was going on, but in retrospect, no one had said anything, except for Ed, who woke me up. Talk about naivety. It was rampant in the Air Force. If the folks back home knew how vulnerable the base was they would have had a heart attack. And to add to that, if the Airmen on the base had a clue, they would have been very nervous, too. I couldn't be the only concerned one out of hundreds, could I? Well, it seemed business as usual. Guys were going to breakfast and to their duty station. Well, I might as well eat.

Chapter 25

The chow hall was at least a mile away from the shooting. Maybe I was overreacting. I joined the hordes going to breakfast, walking the roads and alleys to the chow hall. There sure wasn't much road traffic on-base. In fact, there was none. No one saw any Mama-Sans around either. Strange. The breakfast line was normal. You signed in, waited in line, picked up your tray...hey -- no Vietnamese serving chow today. Just G.I.s. Very strange. The food was great. After chow, I figured I'd go to my duty station. That meant a long walk, so I started out.

One of the roads to my duty station was like a main road; a hot top, two lanes wide with a sidewalk. I knew it well because it was on this road, when I was first stationed at Tan Son Nhut, that I was grabbed for having the wrong head cover on. It was right by the basketball court. Well, new day, right cover. I was on the sidewalk and about 30 feet in front of me was a couple of guys going to work the sidewalk was cement and built up with the roadway. Along the sidewalk was a ditch. We called it a bingo ditch. In the rainy season, all the sewers and the like ran into these ditches. They were about six feet deep and ran next to most walkways. They were full of water and the like in the rainy season and dry the rest of the time. It was dry now. I noticed the guys in front of me jump into the ditch. For a moment, I thought they were screwing around, but then, my attention was drawn to the sidewalk in front of them. It was just like in a John Wayne movie; I could see bullets chewing up the sidewalk, headed right for me. It even sounded like a movie, only it wasn't. I couldn't believe it. Here I was, in the middle of the base, and coming right down the sidewalk was machinegun or automatic rifle fire. I was in the ditch in the blink of an eye. I didn't have a scratch, but I didn't have a weapon either. No one did. This was absurd. The ditch was deep enough so that whoever was firing at us could not see into the ditch. That meant that they had to be on a low plane, even with the road, and not shooting from one of the buildings around the area. That would have put them at a higher elevation so they could shoot at an angle down into the ditch.

I stayed put for a few seconds then started to crawl up the ditch. I passed the two guys that were in front of me. They didn't have a clue as to what to do and were just sitting there like lambs waiting for the slaughter. I asked them if they were okay. And they said yes, and that they were staying put. I crawled about one hundred feet and saw there was a pipe under a side road that branched off the one I was walking on. I crawled through the pipe and came upon an Air Force security officer laying in the grass on my left. He had an M-16, and said he didn't know where the shooting was coming from. He had a portable radio with him and was talking to someone on it and other than that, he didn't have a clue as to what to do. I didn't want to stay in the ditch, because if the shooter changed position so he could shoot down the ditch, we would all be sitting ducks.

There were buildings and barracks all around the road, and I figured the shooter had to be on the right side of the road. If he was on the left (our side) he wouldn't have to show himself to change position to shoot down the ditch. He must have been on the right and didn't want to expose himself by running across the road to our side. He must have seen the security officer with the M-16, because no one else had a weapon. He would have seen that when he sprayed the sidewalk. I figured that I was crawling towards him, but there was no way he could see me. I just kept crawling and when I got into some buildings I would de-de (Vietnamese for rush) out of harm's way. And that is exactly what I did.

I went through some yards to some of the Vietnamese homes that were part of the base and was wondering if the owners were involved in any way with the shooting on the road, and if I was headed into more trouble. I heard some more small arms fire and had my doubts that I could get the mile or so back to my duty station. I decided to head to the only place I knew, where someone with some authority and knowledge of what the hell was going on would be. I ended up running across the street by the base hospital and into the office of my first Sergeant. I told him I couldn't get to my duty station due to sniper fire on-base. He just looked at me for a long second and said, "Forget it. Nothing is moving anyway." We both knew that the whole base was as naked as jaybirds outside of the base security police that at this time were overwhelmed. He was answering the phone and I was just hanging there with no other place to go. After one of the calls, he asked me if I could get to BEMO, draw out a weapon, then get to my hooch and put together a squad of men to be used

158

to augment base security. I was then to bring them to an alley and meet a security police officer to pick up weapons and assignments. I said, "Yes," and off I went.

Chapter 26

The base hospital area seemed secure. I went down that road, then had to go right and pass the main supply area. It was a huge building with a roof but no walls. There were boxes and what we called "conexes" everywhere. A conex is a metal storage container that was used for anything and everything in the Nam. They made great cover as I followed the road to the Bks area. Looking up the road about 50 feet, I saw a base security officer laying on the ground with his M-16 pointing down a ditch. I didn't want to spook him and get shot, so I yelled I was coming up beside him. I ran up and flopped beside him and asked what was up. He said the brass figured the VC would infiltrate the base by using the drain pipes, so he was covering this one. There were hundreds of pipes all over the base and the thinking was right, but this poor guy was all alone. It was plain to see that there was not enough security on the base. It was strange. I saw that the first day on the base and I didn't even know what was going on then. I had been in country three months and nothing had changed until today and now it was too late. I told him what I was up to and he said he could see right down the street and it was clear, so off I went.

I made it into the barracks area from the back, so I didn't have to go on the city side. I got to my hooch and most of the guys were there. Nothing was said to me. I told them I was looking to put a squad of men together as augmenters for the base security force. They all volunteered. I tried to explain that this was for real and then gave some pointers on how to seek cover when we stopped moving. They paid attention and were happy that they could finally do something that meant something. We fell out and made it back to the lonely security officer by the drain pipe. I would have loved to have left a man with him because he shouldn't have been there alone, but we still had no weapons and I wasn't going to leave one of my men there with a handful of rocks. So we left him alone, and I told him I would try to get someone to give him a hand as soon as we picked up our weapons. I could see those words helped him somewhat. There were two or three pipes in the area he was trying to cover, and he knew that if they came up a pipe he wasn't able to cover, he would be hard pressed to stop them. He had a radio with him, but he knew what we all knew.

There wasn't any help available. He stayed and was doing what he was told. Another brave soul. He was all alone and knew it. It now amazes me how in the service your life could be on the line, and you just say, "Yes Sir," and do it.

My squad formed up on me as I was trying to figure out where it was the first shirt told me to report. As best as I could remember, it was right by base supply at one of the huge conex boxes I had come by. The nine of us were working our way around the boxes to stay out of any open areas. I thought the guys were great. They were following my directions and using common sense, something that a lot of people don't have anymore. We came to the center of the supply area, a large open space. I stopped in the shadows and everyone froze as I looked around the area. We had to get across the pad to the base hospital side. I figured it would still be safe on the other side.

I was just about to continue across the open area when I thought I saw a movement. I stayed frozen. There was a shadow of someone in the far corner of the pad that was about 75 feet across and 100 feet long. Forklifts unloaded trucks in the area. Nothing else moved, but I was sure someone was up at the end of the pad in the shadows. I didn't know who it was, but if they had a gun and were not friendly, we would all be in a world of hurt, or worse. I thought of sending one man back to the base security officer by the ditch, but then the culverts would not be covered, and if he was worth his salt, he wouldn't leave his post, and he would be correct, so that was out. He had a radio, but we knew there was no help to be had. I put it to the guys that we would retreat and go around by a road, the same way I had gone down to the hooch. I sent one of the guys back to the security officer to let him know that there might be some unfriendly people on this side of him so he could get into a better defense position. We would wait for the runner to return before we went up the road. He came back in short order and off we went.

We made it to the Base Hospital road and at the end was a Sergeant from Base Security. He was standing by a conex and was happy to see us. He opened the locked conex and it was full of M-16's. We each drew a weapon and a small amount of ammo. Some of the guys didn't even have helmets so they were sent to BEMO to get them. The security officer said he was splitting us up. I didn't like the idea, but he was in charge. I guess his reason was that he wanted the green troops with more seasoned security police. I had doubts about just how knowledgeable some of those leaders were. So, I lost my squad.

Chapter 27

Being that my duty station was by the flight line, I was told to report to the civilian air terminal at the other side of the runway. I was informed that a defense position was being set up there. The brass was sure the V.C. were going to make a push for the terminal and that would give them a straight shot right up the runway to any aircraft that was left on-base. I think most of the big stuff had flown out to parts unknown. The runway was like a main road right to T.S.N. I was told the end of the runway was already under attack by ground troops. The only way to the terminal was back toward the hooch where I started with my motley squad. I started out alone this time, but now I had a rifle and 40 rounds of ammo. It wasn't much ammo and I didn't have any grenades, but it was something.

For some reason, I remembered the hospital area at Da Nang. When the wounded came in, they would just strip you and throw everything into a pile. I remember how for some reason, I wouldn't let them have my helmet, but they took everything else. Well anyway, I figured I'd go to the hospital and see if I could get some more ammo from the wounded. I knew it was pretty secure, and I knew that there had to be some wounded with all of this fighting going on.

I got to the hospital in short order and told the first nurse I saw that I needed ammo. She directed me to the pile of web gear taken off of the wounded as they came in, and can you believe that all the wounded brought in were Marines! I figured this because all of the web gear and ammo pouches on them were 7.62 cal ammo for the M-14 rifle. It did me no good, because I had the M-16. It was a very different type of ammunition from what I needed. I couldn't believe it. So, I left the hospital enroute to the flight line, for some reason I wasn't thinking right because I didn't pick up any grenades from the web gear I went through and there were plenty there I just wasn't thinking.

I was very familiar with the roadway by now. It wasn't long before I came up to the lone security officer by the drainage ditch again. I told him how our asses were hanging out in the wind and that no help will be available. I stayed with him for almost an hour to make his position bearable. He was more relaxed when I had to leave him for the

166

third time. He thanked me and we wished each other good luck. I never saw he again hope he made it okay.

There was constant small arms fire with some heavier stuff mixed in, but not much. I had to get back by our barracks compound then hang a left up a ramp or roadway to the runway. The ramp I had to go up was nicknamed "Charlie row." It was rumored that in the past, the V.C. would threaten this ramp so much trying to get to the runway that they almost owned the thing. One good aspect was that this was one place that had above ground sand bagged foxholes. I made good use of them and didn't see another soul.

I had to stick to the right to get to the civilian side of the runway and the terminal. As I got closer to the civilian terminal, I came upon some bodies: some V.C and a couple of G.I's. I checked the soldiers and they were gone. It must have been a short firefight during the night. After seeing up close what small arms fire can do to flesh and bone, I swore right then that I would never hunt again. It isn't like the old cowboy movies I watched as a kid. It isn't nice. I picked up two more clips of ammo, but still no grenades.

I reported to the civilian terminal at about fifteen hundred (3 o'clock p.m.). There was a security police officer in charge of about a squad size detachment in the front, approximately nine or ten G.I.s. There were more men stationed in the back facing the runway. I don't know how many. The building was two or three stories, but we never got off the first floor. I guess the reason being that if we lost the first floor, anyone above would be a lost cause. I disagreed; it is always better to have elevation in shooting, but I didn't have any say in the matter. The whole protection of the base was boiling down to the low man on the totem pole making the decision of what to do. It was turning into a cluster mess, if you know what I mean.

The big MAC V compound, the building I first reported to, was across from us, and we all knew they had plenty of protection. We were constantly told not to fire toward MAC V. If we did, they would in turn think the V.C had taken the terminal and unleash all the firepower they had back on us. That would be a friendly fire storm and no one wanted that. Here we were, right in the middle of a residential area with shooting all around us and there was no plan or anything. It was just hanging around and waiting. We had no water or chow, but no one was thinking about it. We started to stack the wooden benches used by the people waiting at the airport for barricades. It was going to be dark and we needed protection. The wooden benches really wouldn't do it, but it was all we had. There was a civilian house made of cement about one hundred feet across the parking lot to our right. MAC V was more to our left. No one had checked the building that I knew of. I was really getting pissed off. All that extra training and I'd make a comment about something and all I got for a response was, "Don't worry about it."

We checked our fields of fire and the surrounding area away from MAC V that we could shoot. With no electricity when it started to get dark, it got dark very fast. It was a little eerie in that terminal with everyone just as still as they could be, and with the dark came the goblins. It first started on the flight line side with a lot of firing. The squad I was in was facing front, and we were all hoping that our back was holding. We didn't need any surprises. I had no idea of the time. It was maybe about 23 hundred (11 o'clock p.m.) and things were quiet all around, so the security officer decides to walk out in front of our positions, behind the benches we had stacked up, take out a hand flare and fire it. It scared the wits out of me and the rest of the guys because we didn't know what he was up to. When fired, it made a pretty good noise and lit up the area as the flare came down on a small parachute. It sure screwed up our night vision and as soon as it went off, we started receiving small arms fire. We didn't know if it was from MAC V or just in front of the building aimed at us. MAC V was protected by Army units and we didn't know how far out from the building they were deployed. Um...what to do?

Chapter 28

I was with a Staff Sergeant one rank higher than I. I told him I thought that the guys at MAC V were worried that flare was giving their position away. We both shot up at the flare, riddled the parachute and it fell like a stone and burnt out on the ground. The shooting stopped. The security officer was mad as hell, but it didn't last long. He left to check the back of the building because there were always some shots being fired there. The Sergeant I was with said we should try and get some sleep and that I should take the first break and he would get me up to relieve him in a couple of hours. I said, "okay," and found a spot on the cement floor and laid down.

I had just got comfortable and started to doze off when I was awakened and told to stand to. A report over the radio from the security officer had said we were going to be hit with rockets and mortars. An attack was always led by a mortar barrage. You sure can't dig a foxhole in a cement floor, so we just waited. We hunkered down behind the wooden benches we had stacked up and waited. It wasn't long before we heard the mortars landing around the base and this time, there was a newer sound: rockets. They were well known in the Nam and were the 122 mm type. From what I had learned in one of the schools I went to, they were very basic. You just make a way to point them in the general direction and fire. They were very inaccurate, but with enough pointed in the right direction, they were bound to hit something and do damage. That night, they must have had plenty. They took out the base chapel, the new Base Exchange was hit, along with some aircraft. We were spared. The terminal was not hit.

Around 06:30 we were told the area was secure and to report for new assignments. The Base security building was back on-base, not far from the basketball court or where the sniper had been spraying the sidewalk on the day before. I walked from the base to the report in area. There was a small parking lot area beside the one story, small cement building. There was about fifty guys standing around and sleeping on the hot top. I couldn't remember the last time I slept, so I put my helmet on the hot top, laid down using my helmet as a pillow and fell asleep.

I was awakened about an hour later and told to get on a truck. We were going out to the far end of the runway as a quick reaction team. I guess even in the daylight we were having problems. I climbed in the back of the deuce and a half and away we went. We went out by the end of the runway, the truck stopped, and the ten of us jumped off the truck. We went with staff Sergeant Moon of the Security Police. This guy seemed to be everywhere and he impressed people with his knowledge of what to do and what was going on. He sure looked beat, but it was nice to see a leader for a change.

Up in front of us, we could see bodies of some V.C. lying by the road around the runway. We were told there were snipers all over the place and every once in a while, they would get together and try to fight their way across the road to the runway. We had to clear up the area and make it secure. We spoke of how the only way to find a sniper was to expose yourself. When he shoots you, someone else could shoot him. That is bad business, and we had to come up with a better way. It seemed they were dug in an area covered with tall grass. With some of us country boys in the team, it was suggested that if the wind was right, why not set the grass on fire and burn the bastards out? "Gee, can we do that?" some of the guys said. Well, I wasn't about to get wasted on some stupid call like we were on right now. It sounded like a good plan to me.

We were lying in a ditch on one side of the road, and the grass was on the other. All we had to do was make sure the wind was right and get a fire started. The wind was right and there were plenty of smokers with lighters. The plan was a go. We would crawl up and down our side of the ditch, start shooting across the road like we were going to storm the place, and one of the guys would slide across the road a short distance from us and start a fire. We did this about six times and the grass started to burn pretty well. We then just laid there and waited. After about ten minutes we started to hear the V.C calling to each other. No one understood the language, but I'd have bet they were asking each other what they should do. We could see some of the grass moving as they crawled through it back toward the perimeter fence they had come through. One or two got up to run and were cut down. There were some buildings by the wire fence, but they weren't in our control anymore, so it didn't matter if they burned. We could see a lot of fires around anyway.

It was about this time I remembered my camera that I had put in my pocket when I threw my flack vest and helmet on. It was a small cheap thing, but I figured I'd get some pictures of the field burning. Well the hamster wasn't running on the wheel in my brain, because I decided to stand up to get a picture and for the first time, I learned that when a bullet is fired at you, it kind of cracks as it goes by. Well anyway, I got back down in a hurry. I did take a picture, but it was from ground level and later, when I saw it developed, it didn't show much.

Chapter 29

We stayed there about five hours and then got picked up and brought back to base security. At base security they took my name again, and told me that I was going to be assigned to what was called a "quick reaction team." I guess that meant that wherever trouble started, we would be sent to counterpunch the problem. I figured that at least I would be occupied and have a job to do. What I didn't like about this whole setup; I never knew any of the people I would be with. I think it was about 15 hundred (3 o'clock p.m.) and I was told I was going out at 18:00 (6 o'clock p.m.) for guard duty. So using my helmet for a pillow, I got about two hours sleep on the hot top next to the building.

At about 5 p.m., I woke up and ate some C-rations that were available. At 6 I was picked up in a jeep and brought out to a mowed, grassy area right next to a high perimeter fence. There looked what seemed to be a six story building with other buildings attached to it, making a city block right across from me, about 100 feet on the other side of the fence. There was already a security police airman there. The jeep left and we were on our own. He did have a radio for communications with him. I asked him where we were going to set up, and he said about ten feet off the fence. I asked if there were any foxholes to be used and he said, "No." We were just to lie down on the grass for the night. I had never heard anything so stupid in my life. There were no sand bags, no foxholes, and no trees. Nothing but a nice mowed grass to lay on with a tall building looking down on us. Give me a couple of Marines anytime. I said, "Fine," but added that I was going to set my ass right here, ten feet off the fence and that when it got dark I was moving to another location. If someone was watching I wasn't going to be where they thought I was. He agreed.

By 8 p.m. it was dark enough for us to move, and we did, about 50 feet away from where we were. I had no idea where the closest bodies on guard were from us, so here I was with one other body lying on the grass watching our front. There were lights on the buildings across the road to our front, so there were shadows everywhere, and that is hard on the nerves when you are watching for people in the shadows. The security officer had a two way radio, and there were constant radio

177

checks. With the lights around and the chatter on the radio, we were very exposed. It was almost like we were there to be seen, not to protect. I can only think, looking back now, how it was all for show on the base and not to serve any real security. It just didn't figure.

At about 01:30, the security officer came up with a packet of chocolate from a C- Rat meal and asked if I wanted some hot chocolate. I said, "Sure." He had an old, empty coffee can that had been used before as a heater. We crawled over behind some bushes, got some twigs and grass, put it in the coffee can and started a small fire in it. We then pulled out our canteen cups that come with our canteens, poured in some water and some chocolate mix and proceeded to heat the cups up on the fire we had going. That was the best hot chocolate I had ever had. It sure hit the spot and kind of broke the tension of the night.

About an hour later, a jeep came by checking all of the outposts. That helped pass the time also. The head sergeant in the jeep asked me if I wanted to go on another security detail that was coming up in about 20 minutes. I said sure, if it was okay to leave this post. It was, so I hopped into the jeep and we headed off into the darkness. I was informed that they needed guards on some busses that were going into Saigon. Again, the famous words hit me: never volunteer. I knew things were not good downtown. It was now the second day of the attack.

I was dropped off by the main gate at Tan Son Nhut. The base was so wide open before the attack; it didn't even have a gate to close across the main road. To fix that, they were moving up large trucks to form a roadblock across the road at the entrance to the base. I was told a bus would pick me up. It was about 3:30 a.m. and still very dark and there was still a lot of small arms fire all over. A huge wrecker was blocking the road just inside the entrance, and the ARVNs (Army Republic of Vietnam) had brought up an antique world war two flatbed truck with a 20 MM cannon on it. It was the same type I had seen on U.S. Navy ships in pictures of WWII. They were used to shoot down planes attacking the ships. In this case, it was aimed at the front gate in case of an all-out ground attack.

A 20 MM is a good size gun. It isn't belt fed in the manner a machine gun is, but it is close. The shells are fed from a large rotary magazine attached to the side of the gun, so it is something like a machine gun, but it has to be mounted on a heavy vehicle due to the tremendous recoil when it is fired. On ships, it was welded to the deck. In this case, it was welded or bolted to the truck body. The gunner is strapped in to the big shoulder supports so he could aim and fire.

It was plain to see the base was in trouble as far as defending it goes. There were no walls around it except for barbed wire fences, no gates to close on the roads into it. Talk about trying to keep up appearances for the press. It was turning into a joke; a very cruel joke. I started talking to some infantry grunts that had been shifted back from the boonies to guard the base. They told me how the Military Police Unit that was stationed in the city really got hit hard and lost a lot of people. One G.I. told me that when the security at B.O.Q. number three called for help, the powers to be sent a load of soldiers down to give them a hand in a deuce and a half truck. The V.C were waiting for them and ambushed them. They didn't have a chance. I just couldn't believe how bad things were. I learned that during the rocket attack, when I was at the airport terminal, we lost not only part of the new B.X. but the base chapel, a couple of warehouses, some two story barracks and other stuff. The only air support seemed to be Army choppers because all the big air bases were shut down due to the attacks.

Chapter 30

The whole world changed in one night. It seemed strange to me that back in November, I was told the brass thought the V.C were up to something, but no one did anything to prepare for an attack (except pull some Army units in from the field to around Saigon -- the problem seemed to be that the attack was coming from Saigon). As I was talking with the troopers, an Army Staff Sergeant came over to me and asked what unit I was with. I had no unit markings, only fatigue pants, combat boots, helmet, M-16 and a flak vest. I had no shirt that would show my rank or unit. It was too hot to wear a shirt so I just wore a t-shirt and my flak vest. A flak vest was standard issue to troops in the field. It was a protective vest that we all wore and could attach grenades and the such It protected the wearer from shrapnel and some small arms fire.

The Staff Sergeant asked what I knew about the area around the base I told him that I didn't know much, but I'd been around it somewhat. He asked if I could give him a hand at setting up some kind of perimeter security just outside the base. He said the base security had all they could do keeping the base intact. The Army had to stop the infiltration before it got to the base. I told him I was to be security on a bus going downtown to a B.O.Q. to pick up some officers. He told me that he didn't think that a bus with one armed guard was going to get very far. He said that just a few hours ago, an ARVN (Army Republic of Vietnam) armed car tried to get to B.O.Q. #3 with ARVN and U.S. Army reinforcements and were driven back under heavy fire. I knew I was headed for a B.O.Q., but I didn't know which one. I did know I wasn't a happy camper. Thinking back I was sure the Sergeant in the jeep said that he needed security for some busses going downtown. He said busses plural, but I was the only one there at the gate waiting for a bus. I think I was conned big time. Yep, never volunteer.

Well, a bus did pull up. It was about 4 a.m., the bus stopped and the driver asked me if I was waiting for him. I said "yes," but there was a problem and I called the Army Staff Sergeant over to talk to him. We found out he wasn't going anywhere near B.O.Q. #3, but to one of the other Hotel B.O.Q.'s. We decided to give it a try and if everything went as planned and I made it back, I would have the driver drop me off just outside the main gate and I would see if I could give him a hand. I got on the bus and thought of the bus in Kansas City and the bus my second day in the Nam. I was beginning to dislike these buses. The driver and I didn't talk. It was pitch black. He was driving as fast as he could without lights and to add to the challenge, the White Mice, or the Vietnamese police (we called them "White Mice" because they were small and always wore white shirts. And the QC which I think was the military police because their helmets always had a big QC painted on them. I don't know what it stood for; (maybe police?) and the ARVNs had blocked all the roads with barbed wire and cement barricades. We would go tearing down a street and take a sharp turn only to find out the road was blocked off what a ride. The driver was great. Man could he drive. I didn't ask him if he had volunteered for this as I had or not, but he was good. I wish I knew his name.

The ride took about 10 or 15 minutes and we pulled up in front of this big hotel and stopped. As soon as we stopped, five or six guys, some in pilot jumpsuits and I think two in civilian clothes, piled on the bus. They all had pistols out and were shouting, "Go, Go!" As we pulled away, a bullet came through the back window of the bus. Then, another through the side and right out the other side. We were lying on the floor and the driver took off like a bat out of hell. We took a corner and were on our way back.

The passengers were all saying how the B.O.Q. was under sniper fire all night. They just wanted to get to the base and away from the snipers and all they had were 38 cal revolvers, a very poor weapon for combat. I figured they had to be pilots because all the pilots I'd seen in the past always seemed to carry the 38 Cal revolvers for a side arm. All other branches carried the great 45 Cal automatic, a much better suited weapon for combat and stopping power. The guys we picked up were really worried. They said everyone seemed to be shooting at the B.O.Q. they lived in. Up until that night, it was party time anytime they wanted at the B.O.Q. Now, they were in a war zone. They couldn't believe the change in one night. None of us could.

I told the driver to stop at the main gate and let me off and he did. I found the Staff Sergeant that I had spoken to before my ride downtown. He said he had an observation post set up just a short distance from the base and asked if I was interested in joining him there. I said, "Sure." It was in the back of my mind that someone would be looking for me, but that no one knew what was going on anyway. I just felt more comfortable with someone that made his living at being a soldier, not a part time traffic cop or security guard. So off we went in his jeep. He even had a driver. From what I saw, he was the ranking officer of the unit, and he was treating me as an equal. Seeing that I didn't have any rank showing, the other guys just took it for granted that I was the other NCO in charge and never questioned anything.

We drove up beside a small two story building on a side street and went inside. There were four G.I.s inside so with the three of us, it made seven. A radio was set up and a hole was blown in the wall on the second deck that was more of a loft than a whole floor. One guy was always watching the street through the hole in the wall. I say "hole," but it stretched from the floor to the roof and part of the roof was gone. The building was once a house, but we were the only occupants. There were bullet holes all over the house, and I figured this was where the shooting I heard on the first morning was coming from.

Chapter 31

It was just starting to get light out and we figured the V.C would begin to disappear as it got lighter, like they always did, and the pressure would be off for the rest of the day. I looked at the radio on the floor they had set up. It was a lot larger than the Prick 25 I carried out of Da Nang. I was talking to the radio operator about it when the house partially fell in from an explosion on the side of it. We all got back up off the floor and checked everything and made sure no one was storming the place. All was quiet, but the jeep we came in was blown up. We felt that it was either a grenade or a R.P.G (rocket propelled grenade). It had to be an RPG from across the street. That meant we had company and that they were planning to either take control of the neighborhood, or to pull out and just wanted to give us a parting shot. No matter what, it wasn't good.

We started looking for any movement as it was getting lighter all the time. There was another explosion downstairs. We were up in the loft, the house was starting to rock and shake, and one of the troopers looking out the hole started to fire his M-16. He yelled that there was shooting coming from a house down the street. We all started to get into position to have something to shoot at. The Staff Sergeant said he had to call in because the last RPG had wounded one of the guys downstairs and he had to get him out.

One of the guys noticed something in the light that no one had picked up before in the darkness; the house across the street had antennas on the roof. That could only mean one thing: radios. It had to be a house being used as a headquarters for the VC. It was right then we saw a car coming down the street, and it had an RPG launcher sticking out the side window. We all knew that the people in the car were headed for us. Everyone in the house started firing at the car it was still about two or three houses up the street when it died. We were pouring so many rounds into that it just stopped and started to burn. No one got out.

We were still getting fired on from across the street and were very busy. The house delivering the fire was similar to the one we were in, but with no windows or holes in the second floor, and the first floor had a kind of porch roof over the front. We had the advantage of elevation on them, and they really couldn't shoot up at us because of the overhanging front roof. I wasn't much help as for fire power due to the fact I only had forty rounds that lasted me about one minute. Once it had been exhausted, I had nothing.

I remembered learning that a G.I. in combat isn't about to surrender any of his ammunition unless he is wounded. That was it; the wounded guy down stairs. I climbed down the ladder from the loft to where he was laying. I crawled over to him and asked how he was doing. He was in shock, pale as could be. Someone had bandaged his side and his legs. It looked like the bleeding had stopped. I told him that it had and that he was going to make it okay. I asked him if I could have his ammo and grenades as he was going to be on Easy Street for a while and wouldn't need them. He gave a faint smile and I told him help was on the way. I didn't climb back up the ladder but instead crawled over to the opening blasted by the second grenade. From this position, I could fire right into the front of the building. There were a lot of bullets coming through the walls down stairs, a lot more than upstairs. I didn't think I would be lucky enough to make it up the ladder without getting shot, so I stayed put behind some rubble and kept firing. After about ten or fifteen minutes it started to die down. It was sheer terror for that time and then it stopped. No one knew if we stopped first or if the house across the street stopped first but it just stopped. I found out that you sure use a lot of ammunition in a short time if you aren't careful. I also found that I no longer had my bad habit of ejecting a live round before I started to shoot. That seemed like a million years ago.

No one was moving, just watching. Nothing was happening. It seemed to be a war of nerves. The Staff Sergeant was on the radio and said a couple armed personnel carriers with troops were just down the street and an ambulance was with them. They were not receiving any fire. We could hear their diesel motors not far off. The ambulance pulled up right in front of our house and not a shot was heard. Of course, with two APC's and about 20 troops, we had plenty of firepower now. I learned that two guys upstairs were wounded also, one in the leg and one in the arm, but they would be okay. The house across the street was empty except for six bodies inside, and it was confirmed that it was a VC headquarters from all the maps and radios in it. The medic with the ambulance told me that the wounded G.I. downstairs with me was dead. Besides his initial wounds, he had been hit by some of the bullets coming through the walls. It was starting out to be a very bad day. The Staff Sergeant was going out with the APC's to continue a sweep of the area, I told him I was going back to base before I was reported missing. He thanked me and we wished each other luck. Before I got into the ambulance to ride back with the wounded, I took some pictures of the car we stopped and the house we had the fire fight with. Refer to page A4

Chapter 32

I rode back to the Main Gate at TSN. It was mid-morning by now and all of a sudden I felt very tired. The ambulance took off to the hospital with his horn blowing to let everyone know it was an emergency. You see in real life, the military ambulances used in the field did not have sirens like you might see in the movies or in old TV shows like M.A.S.H. In real life, the driver only had the vehicle horn to get people out of the way or to get the M.P.s to clear the way for them. I made my way back to the Base security shack and was told to report to my unit for further orders. No one ever missed me. I think it was the third day of the attack. Anyway, I reported back to my first Sergeant and told him I had been released from augmentation duty. He told me to go get some rest, so I went to my hooch and laid down. I was so exhausted. I just fell on my rack and went to sleep.

It was dark when someone was pulling me and telling me to get up. There was a rocket attack on and I had to get under cover. Where? I didn't know. The hooches weren't sandbagged like on a Marine or Army base, but I got out and laid in the grass by the hooch. I fell back asleep in the grass and woke up in the morning. When I got up, I raided the last of my stash of C-Rats for chow. Coming back from the head (bathroom), I was advised that everyone in the squadron, along with all the other squadrons on-base, would be on sand bag detail. All of the buildings were now to be sandbagged at least four feet up all sides. I kind of chuckled and thought: well, the horse is out of the barn now. Anyway, there were details filling sandbags, placing them on flatbed trailers, bringing them to the hooches and buildings on the base, and others taking the bags off the trailers and placing them around all the buildings.

Well, that assignment lasted one day. I was then called, along with about twenty other troops, to the first Sergeant's office. We were told, in typical government fashion, that there was not enough sand on-base for the sandbags, so we were being assigned as sand truck security detail. I couldn't believe it, but to bolster the local economy, the government had given a contract to the Vietnamese to truck in sand from a huge sand plant somewhere up Rte. 1 back to the base. We were to ride as guards to protect the trucks hauling the sand. I couldn't believe that I was going to be risking my life to protect a truck load of sand. We all would. We were told the drivers would not make the run without armed guards. All the guys on this detail knew that the drivers were smart. Number one, if there was trouble, they were protected. Number two, if the V.C. were watching, the drivers could say, "We had to haul the sand. Look, they had armed men riding with us to make sure we did as we were told." They couldn't lose. And on the upside, the government was paying big time for the trucks. So, all of us that were riding shotgun were not in a very good position. We figured that at least one half of the drivers were V.C.

I remembered the first convoy that I rode in going to Long Binh my first day in country. All of the trucks had guys riding shotgun in every one, but they were regular Army trucks, and just about everyone had a weapon. We were going to be one man to one truck with a Vietnamese driver that did not speak English. We soon learned that the trucks we were going to be in were very small dump trucks with a regular cab. No open tops where we could stand up and have a good line of sight. We were just sitting ducks in the passenger seat. This war to me was just getting more bizarre by the day.

The next morning, the trucks were at the main gate. We each picked a truck, they were all the same except for color, and hopped into the cab. When I say small trucks, I mean small. They weren't ten wheel dump trucks like you see going down the road today, or trailer dumps like you see, no, these things were very small trucks, just a little larger than the real big pickup trucks you might see on the road. In fact, the truck I chose was a Dodge dump truck. I didn't even know they made them.

We started out as a convoy of about fifteen trucks. It took about, I guess 30 to 45 minutes to get to the huge gravel plant where they were making the sand. Now, get this, the plant would not allow any soldiers into the plant. Can you believe that? We were made to get out of our trucks so they could enter the plant and get loaded with sand, then we were to get back into the trucks when they came out loaded. I guess that explained why we couldn't use military trucks to haul the sand. I guess we were buying the sand from the V.C. Talk about supporting your enemies. We sure were.

Once your truck was loaded, you left for the base. That meant we were no longer in a convoy, just one truck going down the road. It also meant we'd be a great target because we wouldn't have the concentrated firepower a convoy would have. We were only one gun per truck, and that one truck was alone. The truck would pull into TSN and dump its approximately five or six yard load at different locations all over the base, and then it was off for another load. The driver always knew where to dump beforehand and never stopped any other place. I didn't see another truck except in passing going into the base when we were going out all day. That first day went without problem.

Chapter 33

That night, after the trucks dropped us off at the main gate at about 17 hundred hours (5:00 pm), I had my first warm meal in four or five days. It sure was good. That night was okay, and I was back in the truck the next morning. Before I got into the truck at the main gate, I was given C-rations to eat and was told that the first day, the V.C were probably just watching us to see a pattern they could use against us, so to be on our toes today. The first trip was normal, but on the second trip to the base, my truck came upon one of the trucks that had been running a distance in front of us, probably 15 minutes. We stopped as it was off the side of the road with not a soul around it. My driver was familiar with the truck, I think, because he seemed concerned, and I was surprised he stopped. It seemed an explosion had hit the center of the truck from underneath, blew the drive shaft and the whole rear end of the driveline differential off and all was facing backwards. I'd never seen anything like it. I remembered the truck going to Cu Chi but the whole driveline of that truck was gone. I mean pieces everywhere, and this was very small and concentrated in a small area. We started down the road, and I figured the load of sand protected the truck very well. As we left, I wished I had taken a picture of it but I didn't.

On our trip to the base, the trucks had to go through a kind of pass with hills on each side of the road where high power lines crossed the road. I kept thinking that if we were going to have trouble, that would be my place to pick, but here I was, sitting in this small cab just sweating out the ride. Our truck was coming up to the pass I had on my mind when a bullet came right through the windshield between me and the driver. I yelled at him to "di di mau" which meant run fast, but it was the only thing I knew in Vietnamese. He knew what I meant and tried to go as fast as the slow truck would go. I couldn't do anything from inside the cab, unless I wanted to shoot through the windshield, but there was nothing to shoot at. That one shot was the only one that hit through the pass.

As we cleared the pass, we came upon a convoy of new armed personnel carriers coming up the road. They were enroute to their new assignments. I think who ever shot at us saw the APCs coming and that stopped any further action. Great luck for us. I did take a shaky picture of that. After that, I started to ride in the back of the truck with my rifle up on the cab so I could respond better. When the truck got going down the road, I would climb out of the cab and swing myself into the body. I would pull off one of the side boards from the side of the truck, stick it into the sand and use it as a seat, just like a stagecoach seat behind and above the cab. The breeze felt good, and I was in front of the blowing sand. It was ideal. As we pulled into the base, I would put the sideboard back and swing back down into the cab. You know when you are young, it was just amazing the things we did without a thought about how dangerous it was.

The next day, when I was sitting on the load up behind the cab with my rifle laying on the truck cab, we fell in behind a convoy coming up to the pass where we got shot at the day before. I sure felt better, and I took a picture of the rise where the shot came from. I also wanted to get a picture of the guy riding shotgun like I was. See Plate 11.

I was on the truck detail for a week and only had to use my rifle once. I think it was the fourth day. I was sitting in the back on my improvised seat. We were going over a bridge and the ARVNs that were guarding the bridge were engaged in a firefight to the left. I think the V.C. were trying to get explosives under the bridge to blow it. The truck stopped and I started shooting up the river a short ways where the ARVNs were shooting. I was up on the truck so I had elevation in my favor and that is a big plus in any firefight. I learn well. It took about ten minutes and then we were allowed to cross the bridge.

Chapter 34

After the truck detail one evening, I got back to my hooch and discovered that it had been sand bagged and a fighting trench had been dug next to it that would serve as a mortar and rocket shelter, and a bunker was being built in the area. Gee, someone was waking up to the real world. We were further advised that there would be sirens around the base to warn everyone of a mortar or rocket attack. It seemed the Air Force was catching on about a war in the area. Things were quiet for a couple of days and the papers were saying we had driven the V.C out of the area. That was nice to see. We had a television in our hooch that played armed forces programs and a few shows a couple of hours a day. There was a short broadcast every hour or so. That really got my attention.

The TV kept showing how to keep your new M-16 rifle clean so it would work. Everyone that got out into the field was hearing about how many G.I.s had been killed because their M-16 didn't work. I had heard the same rumor when I was at Da Nang a month ago, only this time it wasn't a rumor. It was a fact. The damn rifle wouldn't work when you needed it the most. This was very upsetting to us. The M-16 is easy to take apart and clean, but when you are being shot at and need it, you don't have time, and a lot of dead soldiers can testify to that. One of the things I liked about the gun was that at the end of the barrel, near the flash suppressor at the end, it had a small three pronged affair that was great for cutting the wire around the large cases of C-rats we got. The full cases, like the one I got at Long Binh, were about 30 inches long by about 20 inches and 8 inches thick. The cases were heavy as I said and you could carry them by the wire around them for short distances until it cut into your hand. But the wire held it all together, and if we didn't have wire cutters, we would just stick the end of our rifle into the wire and twist. It snapped the wire just great. We were always told not to do it, but it worked just great.

Well, the outcry about the faulty weapons eventually became known at home from the letters being sent by all the G.I.s. There soon was a newly designed M-16 being issued. They had a plunger made into the side of the gun, so if it failed to feed a round, you could use your thumb and push on the plunger to feed the round. It worked somewhat but it was kind of strange.

Most of the new M-16's made today still have that plunger. Also, to our dismay, the new weapons now had a ring around the flash suppressor at the end of the barrel. There was no more using it as a wire cutter. I kept my old issue M-16 right to the end. I never was issued a cleaning kit for it, so I made one up.

Things seemed to be returning back to a normal routine. I had my rifle standing up against my locker in the barracks, and I had noticed I was the only one with a weapon in the place. I was thinking I was supposed to turn it in, but I didn't like that idea, as I had been there before. So before anyone could get any ideas about my rifle, I moved it and stood it up between the wall and my locker so it didn't show. I figured out of sight, out of mind. It turned out I was right. We would get hit with mortars or rockets once or twice a week, and it kind of became routine. We wouldn't go to the bunkers unless it got close, and they say you never even hear the one that gets you. I remember one night lying on my rack and Samack came in. It was about midnight and someone asked him if anything was going on. I can still hear his answer as clear as if it was last night. He said, "Some shit hit around the main gate but not much else." Now, you have to appreciate that the main gate was only about two hundred yards away from us, but it was getting to be so normal, it didn't even rattle us. We left that to the new guys. It makes me think of my first night when the artillery was outgoing and I headed for the bunker. Well, I'd come along way baby as the saying goes.

Chapter 35

It was a couple of nights later. We were all in our racks late at night when a rocket or two got a little too close for comfort. Dirt and dust was everywhere. Some sand bags were torn up and there was a big fire not far from the hooch. And leave it to meat head Samack, he starts singing a popular song of the day, and we just all cracked up and started singing, "Trying to set my night on fire." It still makes me laugh.

The days started to get dull for me. It was about the middle of February 1968, and I was really finding it hard to unwind after being so, well it is hard to explain, just that I couldn't settle down. I mean back at the house in Saigon, the guy next to me was dead. I didn't have a scratch. The two guys upstairs were hit, and that was where I was, but then I was downstairs without a scratch. Now, it was go back to eat, work, take a shower, when they were working, and stay in your own little world. Then on the 18th of February it all started again.

If you ask the average person old enough to remember Vietnam about the TET offensive, they will say that oh, that was the last big push of the Communists in Vietnam. Well, you can tell them they are wrong. It started, like I said, on February 18. We were hit with a huge rocket and mortar attack. I grabbed my gear rifle and headed to the first Sergeant's office. It must have been about 3:00 a.m. and on my way to report in, I had to pass one of the new two story barracks in use. It had taken a hit right through the roof into the top floor. Man, those guys didn't have a chance. Ambulances were already there taking out the wounded and dead. I could see that the flight line was burning bright. That meant they had hit some planes. They sure burn, and if they are the support aircraft with guns on board, you sure could hear the ammunition cooking off from the heat. I was glad I wasn't a fireman.

I got to the Sergeant's office and there was another guy that had reported in. The Sergeant grabbed us and thanked us for reporting in so fast. He said that the ARVN unit that had taken over security of the Civilian airport terminal was having problems. There were snipers trying to break through to the runway. Sound familiar? Anyway, they needed, of all things, flashlight batteries. My unnamed buddy and I were told what conex box to go to and get as many cases of batteries as we could carry and a van would be in front of the first shirts office to pick them up when we got back. It was a simple job: go down some alleys about a quarter of a mile, pick up some boxes and hustle them back. A quarter of a mile isn't very far, but now add pitch dark, a rifle helmet, and ammo. Oh, and drop a few rockets around to make it interesting. Well, off we went.

We ran and stopped beside a truck and grader that had been parked randomly around the base for quick use. Things were scattered so they couldn't all be targeted at once. We got our bearings and found the conex and grabbed some cases of batteries. Off we went, retracing our route. It probably took about five minutes to get back to the truck we had stopped at on our way out and as we approached, a rocket landed between it and the grader . It blew us off our feet. We saw a new truck suddenly become second hand. Another thing about real life that Hollywood can't show and that is concussion. The explosion knocked us down and gave us a dirt shower, but the concussion from the explosion so close to the truck just made it junk. The windows were gone, the hood was blown right up from the force, the grader tires were going flat and oil and fuel was leaking everywhere. We got up, looked at each other as to say we are good and started off again. I never learned that guy's name, and he never knew mine, but we did what was asked. Until now, no one ever knew that happened except me and him. I went back the next day and took a picture of the truck. I'll enclose it in these pages. See Plates 15 & 16.

When we got to the office, a van was waiting. It was the Ford Econoline van of the day: windows all around with double doors in the back and two seats up front. We threw the boxes in and the driver asked, "Which one is going with me?" We looked at each other and I said, "I will," and I jumped in. I never saw the guy that went with me again.

It was still pitch black out and I knew we were back on the base, so it was pretty secure. We couldn't go up the flight line like I did the first day of TET because it was all burning aircraft, and if any more rockets were coming, they would be aimed there. So here I was again, riding shotgun. We had to go out the main gate and to the civilian terminal from the civilian side. We were going slow as we came up to the terminal, and I could see that a lot of Navy personnel were in the terminal waiting for the plane home in the morning. Their year was done. I was looking at them with envy as we passed by.

The ARVN complex we were going to was past the terminal and now in one of the houses I was so worried about a lifetime ago. We found it and because a rocket had cut the power, they required the batteries. We unloaded and headed back. It was then that one of the saddest things that happened to me in the Nam happened. We were coming back by the terminal and came upon a scene that I've got to live with the rest of my life.

A rocket had landed right in the middle of all those sailors waiting to go home.

I don't remember it bothering me then as much as it does now. It was probably due to the urgent need for help, and the shortage of time with so many wounded and no help available. Doors were being torn off their hinges to make stretchers. Anything and everything was used. The wounded on their makeshift stretchers were placed on the hoods of jeeps and driven to the hospital on base.

Those guys were just waiting to go home. It was just the fall of the cards as they say. That was a rough night, emotionally. It has bothered me more than anything I have ever encountered.

Chapter 36

When daylight came, all was quiet, and it was back to normal. I think the date was the 18th as I said, because it is written on the side of my helmet, my unofficial diary. I had started just writing places, but then when it got personal, I started writing dates. The dates start January 31st through the 4th. Then again the 18th through the 22nd and on into May and so on. The last date is June 21st. That must have been close to the day my luck ran out. After the 18th, we were getting hammered every night with rockets and mortars and I was back on guard duty at night.

One night, I was with a base security officer and we were stuck living in a sewer ditch for the evening. The smell and conditions were awful to say the least. We had C-rats, but that was one night, no matter how hungry I was, that I couldn't eat. I remember it was the night I was introduced to "Puff, the Magic Dragon." We were right on the perimeter of the base in our ditch and there was one hell of a firefight just a short distance from us when all of a sudden, the sky lit up just like a volcano with flowing lava, only it was right in the middle of a black sky, about two thousand feet up. I had heard about the new weapon, but hadn't seen it yet. I guess it was officially called a C-47 Spooky. It circled an area at night and had what was called "mini guns" aimed out the side of the aircraft. They fired thousands of rounds in minutes and destroyed everything on the ground. It fired so fast it didn't even sound like a gun shooting. It was just a " Whir" sound. At night, it looked like a solid stream of fire just starting in midair and headed for the ground. You see, in any machinegun, about every fifth round (bullet) is a tracer round that burns as it is fired. That way, you can follow it to where it hits and adjust your aim accordingly. With the mini gun, it fired so fast that it looked like every round fired was a tracer. It was awesome to see and the devastation was total. I was glad when that night was over.

A couple of days later, I had guard duty with my friend Wagner. It was outside the base near Camp Hoang Hoa Tham. It was the ARVN Airborne School. I don't remember why or how we ended up there, but there we were, sitting in a foxhole when a plane flew over and started dropping parachutists. So, we sat and watched. They weren't very far away and there was a light breeze so they were scattered all over as they came down. As we watched, one of the parachutists started floating towards us, and he was swinging back and forth. It looked like he was trying to get turned around. Just before he hit the ground, a gust of wind kicked up and slammed him into a tree about 20 feet off the ground, and he just dropped like a rock. He wasn't very far away, so we ran over to him lying on the ground.

We didn't know Vietnamese but we could tell he sure was in pain and he was pulling at his harness trying to get it off. We looked at each other and then at the big silver buckle in the middle of his chest that held the harness together. Well, Wagner being the quick thinker he is said we should get him out of the harness and that he knew how. So, he bends over this suffering soldier and with all his might slams his hand down on the silver buckle in the middle of the guy's chest. As he did, that he said very authoritatively that you have to hit this to release it. "Oh!" dummy me says. Well, about the time Wagner's hand contacts the guys chest at warp seven, it occurs to us that he probably has a broken rib. The poor bastard yelled so loud that in no time his friends were there. They reached down, turned the buckle, unhooked his harness and called for an ambulance. Wagner

213

just couldn't understand why they never thanked us. Well, it passed the time.

While I am on the subject of Wagner, I'll mention that he was always doing stuff like that and always with the best intentions. There was the time he found an old ice pick somewhere. He found out that if he stuck it into a sandbag and pulled it out the pick stayed in the sandbag and he just had the handle in his hand. No big deal, it was just an ice pick, but not when it comes to passing the time. Well, Wagner is talking to his buddy and showing him how the ice pick comes apart, all well and good, but then they get the idea of jumping a guy that owes one of them money and threatening him with the pick until he pays up. So, they end up jumping the guy. Wagner waves the pick in front of him and says he is going to stab him because he never paid back the money he borrowed. Well, the pick waved gave the right effect, the pick stuck into sandbag gave the right effect, and pick pulled out of sandbag gave the right affect, only this time, the pick didn't pull apart as planned and the result: buddy stabs friend in chest. They had a hell of a time telling the medic how the guy fell on the pick while walking. It all turned out okay. There was a slight wound, no more debt to be paid off, and he made

214

a full recovery. Still friends. Well like I said, it passes the time.

Chapter 37

Things were getting into a routine. There were mortar and rocket attacks at night and regular duty during the day. It was easy to figure out if anything big was about to happen because if anything big was coming, like a heavy mortar or rocket attack during the day, none of the Vietnamese would show up to work on the base. They knew before we did.

I was still assigned to the security detail on the QRT team (Quick Reaction Team). One day, I was assigned to a three man security detail for what was called "R.M.K.B.M.J. Company." I was told it was a construction company located on the outskirts of the base. There were a lot of rumors that the letters were the names of the owners and they were getting all the contracts around the Nam to rebuild everything. It was all civilian employees and they were all making all kinds of money. The big rumor was that the last letter J stood for Johnson, the last name of the president. I never knew for sure, but it was easy enough to believe. Anyway, I was assigned a truck going out to the construction camp. I was to get the truck at the main gate where it was being loaded with Vietnamese day workers. It was a long flatbed truck with wooden sides. I hopped up into the back then the local workers started piling in. I would have guessed the truck could probably hold fifty people in the back. They must have put over one hundred people in that truck. I was packed in so tight, I couldn't move.

At the construction site, we unloaded and each of the workers went their own way. One of the other security guys was already there at the gate into the complex. He said he was all set as he had a roof for shade and a chair to set on. I was told to wait for the other grunt, and we were to patrol the perimeter of the camp. Well, another truck pulled in, and who got off it but my friend Wagner. We talked over how we would work the security and started to check the place out. It was just the basic construction yard with a lot of heavy equipment around.

It was kind of a gravy job for us. The American civilian employees in charge of the locals had their own office and chow hall that we could all eat in at noon. It was daylight. There was barbed wire and a huge security fence around the whole place, so not bad. Wagner and I figured we would alternate point man on checking the fence. Just inside the fence, there was a low ditch that we could use most of the time for cover. It had water in it, but not much and it was better than walking next to the fence as a target. Right on the outside of the fence, there was tall grass right up to it. We didn't like that, but what can you do. In the middle of the compound was a high watch tower we could climb up in and see the whole place. We started out and I had my camera so I took a couple of pictures and it was just another day. A small convoy of armed personnel carriers went by on the road in front of the complex, so with those around, we felt pretty good.

After one sweep of the perimeter, we decided to climb up the tower to look around. It was pretty high and once up there we could see the whole compound but not much else, because of the bushes and small hills around. We were sitting up there looking around, when all of a sudden all kinds of machinegun and small arms fire started up. There was only one other guard and he was on the gate into the compound. It had to be him. The tower didn't have any sandbags, so bullets could go right through it. We decided to bail out, but it was a long ladder to climb down. Down we went.

Man, that was the fastest I ever went down a ladder without falling and we made it. We headed for the gate and when we got there, we found our companion down off his shelter and chair lying on the ground. We ran up to him. He hadn't fired a shot, but the amount of fire that was going on around us was outrageous. Nothing was coming into the compound. I must of aged ten years in five minutes. We were then informed by one of the civilians that the base firing range was right next to the compound, and the APCs we saw were over there zeroing in their weapons to make sure they could hit what they aimed at when the time came. I figured the civilians got a good laugh at our expense.

It was just about noon so I was going to go to the chow hall and eat, and Wagner would patrol the perimeter, then we would switch and he could eat. I went in the building to eat and a lot of the Americans were in eating too. I noticed that I was like a young kid next to them. I mean, they had to be like in their 30s or better, but the money they were making was out of this world. I ate and they had the best of everything, even ice cream. Man, I couldn't believe it.

I was waiting in a short line for some of that ice cream when we all heard an explosion not very far away. Now, all the old timers were asking me what it was. I thought it was a mortar, but that it had probably landed about two hundred feet from us and was nothing to worry about. I had a helmet on and was carrying a rifle so they figured I knew what I was talking about. I finished my ice cream and went out to relieve Wagner. I found him setting on the ground a short distance from the chow hall. He didn't look too happy. When I got to him, I asked if he was okay. He related to me what had happened. As we had agreed, he was checking the perimeter. As he walked across the compound, a mortar landed right behind him and blew him off his feet. The dirt in the compound was so hard, the mortar only blew a small hole in the ground. He showed me, so I took a picture of him setting in the crater it made. That is one of the few times he didn't have his smile on, when I took that picture. We both knew it was just luck. If he had stopped to light a cigarette or tie his boot along the way, that round would have had his name on it. We also knew that a mortar round wasn't aimed at him. One man doesn't draw mortar or rocket fire. It was just a random shot as always. It just happened to be where he was working. Luck of the draw.

The day ended and we went back to the base, but we were all feeling a lot older. I finally reported back to my duty station on the flight line, and I was advised that the praised jeep we had from Long Binh was destroyed during one of the attacks. Nothing, good or bad, lasts forever. The good news was that we now had what was called an M274 one half ton mechanical mule. The Marines were the only units in the Nam that had them as far as I knew, and I had seen them outside Da Nang. The Mule was a very small platform that had an engine under the rear deck. It drove like a car and had one seat: no cab or protection of any kind. It was about eight feet long, four feet wide and about two feet off the ground. The tires were a bit larger than wheelbarrow tires and with its four wheel drive, it could go anywhere. The top speed was about 12 m.p.h. It started by pulling a rope like a lawn mower in the front. There were no lights and the operator could swing the steering wheel down and when need be, crawl beside the Mule and steer it at the same time. It was some rig. The biggest down fall was the slow speed over the road, but now at least we had transportation again. Where it came from, I didn't know or ask.

It was a tricky vehicle to start. First, you had to stand in front of it, turn a switch, pull out the choke to the engine, and make sure the standard transmission was in neutral. Then, you needed to pull the starter rope until it started. With the choke closed, the small engine would rev up so that once it was running, you could open the choke and it would idle down. It seemed strange to me that even though it was always hot in the Nam, we still had to choke the thing, but it always started on the first or second pull. I really didn't drive it much because it was so slow I felt that I could walk just as fast. Well, almost.

Chapter 38

One day, I was with a guy named Tobey, a newer guy, and the Sergeant that was with me on the trip to Long Binh when I got the C-rats and another Sergeant that was the gunner in the back of the truck. We were talking about current events and what was going on in the world when someone said, "Do you hear that?" We listened and it sounded like tires spinning on pavement, like when someone scrubs out with a car. It was something you didn't expect to hear where we were, only this sound kept right on happening. It kind of got our attention, so we started to look around for it. We couldn't believe what we found. It was a Sergeant from another unit that we knew was going to take the Mule for a ride to pick something up. Well, he did all the starting procedure correct, except for one thing; he didn't make sure the Mule was in neutral, so when it started and revved up, it was in gear and took off. Well, the Sergeant starting the Mule was in front of it, of course. He ran backwards trying to get out of its path, but he wasn't fast enough. The machine pinned him against a wall and ran right up his body. When we found him, the front of the Mule was on his chest, and the back tires (that were still turning from the engine that was still running) were spinning on the concrete sidewalk trying to finish the job of crushing him. The switch that the poor guy couldn't reach was turned off, and we pulled the thing off him. He was in pretty rough shape. He was bleeding from his nose and mouth and was exhausted, but wouldn't go to the hospital. We tried to comfort him and he left for his hooch. It was just an unfortunate accident. The Mule wasn't damaged in anyway. After that, we all paid attention to make sure it was in neutral when we started it.

The Mule had another part of my life in the Nam. Tobey, the newer guy that was with us, was qualified to drive the Mule and came up with an idea to pass the time. It all started one day when he was watching some of the fighters land on the runway. He noticed that most of them deployed a parachute to slow them down when they landed. A lot like the modern day dragsters of today after they have completed a quarter mile run. Well, Tobey noticed that to deploy the main chute, a small pilot chute was used to pull the main chute out. The hamster was running on the wheel in Tobey's brain this day. Tobey somehow got one of

224

the small pilot chutes all packed and ready to hook to a main chute. With his plan, he didn't need the main chute. One day, Tobey pulls me aside and tells me his plan. He explained that he needed help, and thought, "Why not Stoddard? He is easy." Story of my life. The plan being that with the parachute attached to the back of the Mule, we would go out on the runway, get up to speed with Tobey driving and I would pull the ripcord to pop the chute open as we tore down the runway, just like a fighter jet coming in for a landing. Seemed like a good idea. I was all for it. Do the words "NEVER VOLUNTEER" sound familiar?

Well, our caper was kept secret and the big day came. I, of course, had my camera. I didn't want to miss an event like this. Besides, who would believe us if we didn't have proof. The day of the famous Mule landing dawned clear and hot. The time for our caper was set for 11 a.m. and we had picked out a taxiway right off the main runway for our debut.

I took some pictures of the chute set up on the Mule. Tobey was to be pilot and I was navigator. We got lined up on our runway and Tobey opened it up. Well, like I said before, the main drawback of the Mule was its top speed, or rather the lack of it. The Mule was maxed out on speed. We were using up runway at a surprisingly slow speed, and I pulled the ripcord. Right then we both thought, "Gee, if this thing opens and drops our speed like it is supposed to, there are no seatbelts on the Mule." The both of us would continue to march at a faster speed than the Mule and be launched onto the very hard runway while the mule continued to struggle down the ramp on its own. Maybe this wasn't such a good idea after all. Well, the Lord protects the weak of mind, and we were saved. The slow speed of the rig prevented the chute from opening and it just dragged behind us on the cement. So I, with camera in hand, snapped away at a colossal event that didn't happen. See Plates 22 thru 25.

We both figured that a lot of people would be looking for us in a short time because we were not authorized to be where we were. The service is funny about things like that. They just don't have a sense of humor. So when Tobey saw a military police pickup truck heading for us, he made a fast about face and headed for an alley in between some buildings that he knew the truck couldn't follow. He had planned a lot better than I would have. Well, the brain hamster only runs so fast for so long. The thing we never thought of was the obvious. Think about it. If someone in your area had the weirdest vehicle you had ever seen, and no one else had one except for the Marines up north, just about anyone would know where the Mule came from. We were fugitives and had to get rid of the chute, and that we did. It is probably still blowing around the outskirts of Saigon somewhere.

We went back and parked the Mule right where we had picked it up, sans chute. We then got together and formed our story, our air tight alibi. The only problem was that I was to surrender an item that was near and dear to my heart. I had to go to my locker and get my treasured Marine utility cap. We then placed the hat (with my serial number cut out of it) on the mule, and walked away. Later on it was discovered that some Marines had seen the Mule and decided to take it for a ride. Then, they left for up north never to be seen again. Those bastards trying to get us in trouble. Well, we would sure keep an eye on it from now on. We can't have things like that happening anymore. Tobey and I sure kept a low profile after that.

Chapter 39

It was just before or around this time that all the losses of all the services, by that I mean people killed, were really mounting up. I know now you hear in the news that 30 U.S. servicemen and women were killed last month fighting terrorists overseas, and the numbers are appalling just because the news says it is, and it is, but we could lose fifty a day and we did on many days. Often we lost even more and it was just casualties of the war. Well, keep those rates for a month or so and the bodies begin to mount up.

The government had come up with a way of handling the dead in the field. It was a thing called a bodybag. You just put the remains in the bag, zip it up and ship it back to the proper authority. The proper authority at Tan Son Nhut was the base morgue next to the base hospital. It became very apparent that the morgue was not equipped to handle the influx of bodies that was coming in. I had to walk by the morgue every day on the way to chow. I never paid much attention to it, only noticing what it was and all the "Authorized

Personnel Only" signs posted at all of the doors. Well, after Tet, every once in a while there were bodybags stacked up outside the receiving door. It was a reminder to all of us going by that all we had to do was make it through our 12 or 13 months and get home. Compared to what we had now, it would all be gravy after that.

Well, as the days progressed, the stacks of bodies were getting larger. Then, one day, I noticed that one of the refrigeration trucks (they were used to keep some of our food supplies fresh) was now running twenty-four-seven outside the morgue and it was filled with body bags. It was an attempt to slow down the decomposition process that was being accelerated as a result of the heat. We had so many metal transportation caskets for all the casualties that they were being placed on flatbed trailers all over the base for immediate use. This was about the time we were all speaking in hushed tones of the odor that was over everything. It was the smell of death. It was on your clothes, on the ground, on your skin, everywhere. It has been called the "sweet smell of death." Once you experience it, you never forget it. We lived with it. Now that I look back with older eyes on the dead I knew and saw, they seem so young. I guess we were, and the young live forever. It never happens to you.

I recall reading that during World War II, General Eisenhower was addressing the troops for the D-Day invasion. They were all lined up listening and he stated that in the coming invasion, it is forecast that two out of every three men will be killed or wounded and with that, each man in line looked to his left and right at the men next to him and said to himself, "Those poor bastards." And that is the way it is when you are young. It never happens to you. That is, until it does. It was called nature's ultimate reality check. The older I get, the younger they all look. We never talked about it much. We on the base had it so much better than the grunts humping the jungles, and we knew it. It would be absurd to complain. That would be like someone back in the world complaining about the big bump in the driveway, when across town, some people didn't have a driveway, or even a house to live in. We had it good.

Time was just something to count for most of the guys. The count that was so important was how many days you had left to go. You were a short timer if you had less than 30 days to go. That was, unless you were the one counting down. If it was you, it could be any amount of days left that your buddies let you get away with saying you were short. Short to your DEROS (Date Eligible for Return from Overseas) date. To me, it meant: Date Estimated Return of States. That was my understanding of the military term. It may not be correct, but to the grunts, that is what it meant. Every once in awhile, you would hear someone yell "Short!" We all knew what it meant and were happy for the guy. Another saying we heard a lot was, "I'm too short for this shit." Meaning that they had been given a dangerous assignment or dirty job to do and figured that their short time left in country would have gotten them out of said assignment. But of course, no such luck. Shit happens.

Well, time was going by for me, but I was no short timer yet. March came and went, then April and I was fine. Things were quiet during the day, just a few small mortar or rocket attacks at night once in awhile. If you weren't where they landed, you were okay. I started drinking kind of heavily. I was bored and had some money left over after I sent my allotment home to my folks and didn't know what else to do with it. I did buy a couple of cigarette lighters even though I didn't smoke. One had a common saying on it that was used often among some of the grunts. It said "Yea, though I walk through the valley of death, I will fear no evil for I am the evilest son of a bitch in the valley." On the other side of the lighter was a map of Vietnam. The other lighter I bought was a Zippo, said to be the best that was plain. On it, I had inscribed my last name, my serial number, "TSN Vietnam 67-68" and at the bottom "377 misfits." That was what we were called at times, because there was no place we fit in.

I was taking note of the routine on base in that if something was destroyed by mortar fire at night, it would be rebuilt the next day as to have the appearance that not much was going on or no damage from the attacks. We all figured it was for the press, to keep everything looking as normal as ever. After all, we are winning the war, aren't we? Life became rather boring. I would go down to Saigon to the U.S.O. once in a while, but there weren't many shows. I went down to the center and did some shopping. Stuff was cheap. I found that most Vietnamese didn't like the Buddhist religion, so to keep the local Vietnamese from bothering me; I bought a real jade Buddha with a gold chain and wore it around my neck. When I went through customs on the way home when I got out of the Nam, I was told Jade was a product of a Communist country and I couldn't bring it into the United States, so I had to toss it.

Chapter 40

May came and on May 6th I found myself back in business. The night attacks had stepped up some. My rifle was pulled out from beside my locker and I was assigned security once again. I felt like I was home, if I may coin a used phrase. A tank the ARVN used that was once at the main gate was going down a road not far from my hooch when a Rocket Propelled Grenade hit it and knocked it out. An RPG, as they were called, was a shoulder fired weapon of limited range. A mortar on the other hand had a lot longer range. This meant that some of the VC were getting up close and personal. Patrols around the base were being set up to keep the bad guys at arm's length, you might say. They were close to the base and were basically a show of strength outside the wire. It was kind of strange because we could walk down to Saigon anytime we wanted. Well, as it has been said before, Charlie owned the night.

We were to patrol only during the day. The joke was "Who's the Boss? We are…during the day. Who's the Boss? They are…during the night." It was getting so bad that units had to clear where they could fire on with the local mayor or village elder before they could shoot. Sounds like the wars we are fighting now. Put the politician out in the field, and we would see how fast the mess would be cleared up. To keep up the appearance that the Vietnamese Army was running the show, a handful of G.I.s would be sprinkled in with the ARVN (Army Republic of Vietnam, in case you forgot). We would patrol a few streets; the ARVN would stop people and check their papers and such, and then head back to the base. It was the same thing the White Mice (Saigon Police) would do, only we were out "in force" as the saying goes.

Time was passing and it had to be right after the 21st of June. It was a normal hot day. The road was hot top with a sidewalk. Traffic was going by. It was midmorning, I think. I remember the ARVN in front of me fell down and grabbed his right leg below the knee. There was a small hole in his pants' leg, so I used my knife to cut the pants up to his knee, and there, lo and behold, was a bullet hole right through his calf. I was thinking it was from an M-16 round, due to the damage to the surrounding tissue. An M-16 hits with such a high velocity that the impact area takes a beating as the round enters the body. Well, this wound was small like an M-16 round was and the skin around it was pretty beat up. I told him he would be okay and he was number one, which meant good in the universal language of G.I.s. (one being good and ten, bad). I put my knife away and tried to stand up, but fell down. I thought one of the other guys was standing over me and I bumped into him. All of a sudden, I felt a million bees stinging me on my side and back, but I couldn't get up. I was dragged into the ditch next to the sidewalk with the ARVN and my flack vest was pulled off me. It felt like a red hot poker was stuck in my side, although I seem to remember it more now than I did then. One of the guys said I had been hit, but I don't know how. I didn't hear anything and I had my flack vest on and it hadn't been hit. I was given a drink of water and told an ambulance was en route for me and the ARVN. I never heard a single shot fired. Looking back it just amazes me of the kindness of the G.I.s I was with, they knew there was a sniper shooting us and yet they exposed themselves and pulled me into a ditch for cover than they tried to make me comfortable and gave me water I remember one of them holding my head so I could drink the kindness was so sincere and we were just kids. They handled me and the other wounded like we were the most important piece of China or Crystal in the world and didn't want to take a chance of hurting us anymore than we already were. There was water that we were laying in and I noticed it was a pink color which was odd, because all the ditch water I had seen was always brown than I realized it was my blood and the ARVN's blood running into the water giving it the pink hue I was seeing The wounded ARVN was looking at the same thing so we just looked at each other with a faint smile and said we were Okay and number one and waited.

The ambulance came and I remember lying on the stretcher and listening to the horn blowing, as I had heard so many times before. We were taken to the base hospital, the same one I visited when I got back from DaNang, and went in looking for ammo the first day of the TET attack. Now, that really was a lifetime ago. I was brought in and that is the last thing I remember until the next day. I woke up and was hooked up to tubes and wasn't going anywhere that was for sure. A nurse (a round eye, boy did she look good) came in. I say round eye, because American women had round eyes and Vietnamese women didn't. It sure was nice to see those round eyes. I couldn't take my eyes off her. She made her way to me and started talking to me. She spoke English with no accent. It was great. She was an officer, but I don't remember the rank. Heck, who the hell would be looking at rank. Maybe I was dead. She sure was nice, and she informed me I was very much alive and well. She said a bullet went in my side by my left armpit hit a rib and broke into pieces. Some came out my back. Except for a cracked rib, it was basically a flesh wound. They thought it was a ricochet as a normal bullet would have gone through me. She further added that I was very lucky. She didn't have to tell me. I had figured that. I guess I was hit by the same slug that hit the ARVN but didn't know it. Just a guess.

Chapter 41

I was released a week or so later on light duty. That meant no duty for me. I was stiff and my side hurt when I raised my arm, so I didn't raise my arm. I had three months to go in country and I had an R&R coming. That meant I qualified for one week at the government's expense to my choice of offered destinations. Some of the choices were Hawaii, Bangkok, Thailand, the Philippine Islands or Australia. I chose Australia and I put my request in. I also was given my dream sheet at about this time. A dream sheet is a government form requesting your choice of duty station when you leave Vietnam. I thought about Missouri, but I couldn't get back in that situation and live. I just didn't think I was that lucky. So, I put in for the New England and New York bases. I felt very tired and wanted to be closer to home. Home sure sounded good to me. And then the paperwork was put in motion for my R&R and choice of duty station. I was beginning to feel short. It starts as a glow from the inside and then grows to a great feeling.

A month later, I was as good as new except for some scars under my left armpit and on my back. It was back to the routine once again. I was waiting for orders on my R&R, and what my next duty station would be. I still had a year to go with Uncle Sam. I no longer wanted to go into the field as the saying goes. I was feeling too old and slow, and how much good luck can a guy have? Was it good luck? I didn't think so laying in that ditch next to the road, but it had to be.

On July 4, 1968 I received a special gift from Uncle Sam. It was my permissive travel orders for Out of Country R & R. I was to report to Camp Alpha Building #4 at 1330 hours 28 July 1968. This detail is so precise because I still have the paperwork. With the orders was a note that all personnel included on this order were to report to the base dispensary, Building 305, at 1900 hours 27 July 68 for the required short arm inspection. It really didn't say short arm inspection, but we all knew that was what it was for. It was a check by a doctor to make sure no one had V.D. If you did, no R&R for you. Also with the orders were all the requirements and conditions of the R&R. Some included having only 40 pounds of luggage, no weapons, and traveling in our uniform, but once in Australia, we had to wear civilian clothes. that would be a first for any of us in at least ten months. Real civilian clothes. Wow. Also, we had to have a minimum of one $125 to be converted to U.S. Dollars, greenbacks. That would be another first to see since I landed in country and had to turn all my money in for the military "funny money." I sure couldn't wait.

So, on 28 July, I left for Sydney Australia until 4 August. The first thing I did when I got my private room in Sydney was get in the shower and just let the water soak the 10 months of dirt out of me. I forgot how good it could feel. Just great. Then, out into the beautiful city of Sydney. Before I got my orders, guys that had been on R&R to Australia would tell me well there weren't any garbage men in Sydney, and when I asked what they meant, and they would just say that I'd find out. Funny saying, I thought, but once I was there I found out what they meant. The city was so clean that it was almost easy to believe that they didn't need garbage collectors. It was food for thought. And I would say the same thing after I got back. It was a great time in a greater city. I remember the bar called "Whiskey A GoGo." It was where all the G.I.s went to party. There was plenty to drink, great looking gogo dancers and it seemed all the girls in Sydney were there and they were beautiful, just like we dreamed about. The women, or should I say girls, were plentiful. I was there one day and one G.I. that had a girl staying with him was going back to the Nam had her move in with me, simple as that. She needed a place to stay and I was available. Just great. The third day, I met two girls that were from New Zealand and on vacation (they call it "holiday) in Sydney, so I spoke to an Army Sergeant that I had met and he took one of the girls and me, the other. We toured the whole city and then the outskirts. It was great. The girl that was sleeping with me had to move on before my week was up and she did just that. Where, I didn't' know. I learned a lot about Australian girls, a bit about New Zealand and then my time was up and it was back to the Nam.

My last night in Sydney, I went out to supper by myself. I guess I was feeling very melancholy about going back, it wasn't a very good feeling. I was very down thinking about it. I was in a small, upscale restaurant sitting by myself. I remember I ordered a great meal as it would be my last good meal for some time. It was about 10 p.m. and I was just about finished when one of the greatest acts of kindness I have ever experienced was bestowed on me. My waiter came over to me and asked if I cared to join a couple who was having dinner not far from where I was sitting. He pointed them out. They were very well dressed and somewhat older than I. I don't' know why, but I said, "yes" and was escorted to their table. I can't remember what their names were, but we introduced ourselves and I sat down. They said that they were watching me and that I looked so sad, they just had to see if I wanted to join them for conversation. My spirits lifted and I felt a lot better. What great people they were. Of course they were Australian. He was a commander in the Australian Navy on leave and the lady was his wife. We sat and talked for hours. I remember the waiter came around at midnight and poured our drinks into coffee cups because their alcohol licenses said they couldn't' serve booze after midnight, so it looked like we were all drinking coffee. I thought that was neat. Well, we finally said goodnight and I had my faith in the human race restored. What great people the Australians are. They just fit the mold of that great country. Fourteen hours later it was back to the war. It went all too fast.

Chapter 42

On my return to TSN, my orders for my next base were in. The dream sheets I filled out turned out to be exactly that, a dream sheet. My orders told me I was going to Laredo, Texas. Not what I had in mind. My thoughts went back to my friend Whit going to Korea not Germany. You just say, "Yes, sir," and pack your bags. I started asking around about Laredo, Texas and what it was like down there. What I was told did not impress me. That it was hot and dirty was all I could get. I couldn't even find out what kind of a base it was. I did know it was right on the border with Mexico, but that was about all. It was a duty station I was not looking forward to.

Now, me being assigned to the Air Force duty station and not the Marine duty station meant that I would leave in country a month sooner than if I was at the Marine base. That seemed lucky for me, for I was pretty well burnt out by the time September rolled around. This also meant that I was an official "short timer" now. I really didn't give a shit about anything. I figured I'd been there and done that if it came to anything in country. There was not much that impressed me when it came to the service, but that was about to change. First for the worse, well, not terrible, just that I was given another duty assignment.

I was taken out of inspection section and put into inventory section. Seeing that I was waiting for my transfer, I had to be kept busy. The service is great at making busy work for anyone that doesn't have anything to do. Inventory meant that I was to go into all the nooks and crannies of the warehouses on the base and account for everything that was listed in said location. It really wasn't all that bad, seeing as I got to go everywhere on base I wanted to check on all sorts of stuff. I found out in no time that if there was a shortage of anything, it was okay. It could just be written off as war loss, and it was okay. And that was usually what it was. I mean, put anything in a building, and then blow the building up. What else would you expect? What caused a problem was if there was an overage of an item. For example, I was counting scopes for rifles used by the snipers in the area. No rifles, just the sniper scope that goes on it. Inventory said we had four available. I counted seven available. That couldn't be. We couldn't have seven. I was told to go back

245

and recount. There could be only four. Well, I went back and there were only four (after I put three scopes in another location) and I reported four scopes as per the records. Okay, then everything is as it should be. I think in the history of the U.S. Government, they have never given anything back. They wouldn't know how. The paperwork only flows in one direction. My boss was happy, and I didn't look like an idiot saying something was there that wasn't. It was just amazing that my father received three great hunting scopes in the mail: one for me, one for him, and one for my brother in-law. Everyone was happy.

Well, inventory was fine for me, how lucky could one guy be and my luck was going to get whole lot better, if you could believe it. All the guys I knew always said they never saw me when I wasn't smiling, but that was just natural to me. I mean, looking back at my life, I did have a lot to smile about. There was only that six weeks or so that I wouldn't even open my mouth, never mind smile, but that was over now. I was always kidded about the spoon I carried on my flack vest for C-rats. I was always ready to eat. I remember how foolish three G.I.s looked laying in the dirt, looking for cover with all that gun fire coming at us at the construction camp that wasn't even that close to us, and Wagner stabbing his buddy with the Ice pick, or smashing the paratrooper's chest when he had a broken rib. That would make anyone smile looking back at that. Then the great parachute caper on the Mule. That was a classic. Even the snipe hunt and the Turtle club a lifetime ago. What a lucky guy I am. Who wouldn't smile?

Well, good fortune would smile on me as I smiled back one more time before I left the country known as the Nam. I was called into the first shirt's office one day and reported to the company commander as ordered. I was sure someone had found out the I had mailed three rifle scopes home and the government wanted them back, but I know the government, and if doesn't exist on paper somewhere, it doesn't exist. I couldn't send three scopes home that didn't exist. Well, that wasn't the reason I was called in. In reviewing the personnel section of my records and pointing them out to the squadron, it came to light that with my time in grade and service and record, I could be eligible for discharge from military service a year sooner than my obligation stated. Wait one, run that by me again? It was true. I had the choice of going to my next duty station, or being discharged from the service when I returned

247

to CONUS. Conus stood for military jargon for Continent of the United States. Everything in the military was abbreviated, to save space in paperwork, and it followed through to the way we talked.

They asked me if I was claiming any disabilities on my termination of military service, if I was to take it. I wanted to go into the law enforcement field after the service, and I didn't want anything on my record that would show I was collecting on a disability for anything so I said "No." I think in the same breath, I said, "I'll get out." I couldn't believe it. I was getting out a year sooner than I thought. How lucky can one person be? So, by the end of August, my orders read "Request and Authorization for Permanent change of Station-Military. 60 Air Base Group Travis AFB Ca.94535. Report to commander, New Assignment NLT (no later than) immediately upon arrival. Special order no AA-6975." I was going home for good.

The last time in the Nam I sweated it out was at the civilian terminal that I had spent the first night of TET in and then later, seeing all the dead and wounded sailors after the rocket hit them. They were waiting to go home just as I was. Needless to say, I was nervous. There were a lot of guys that were in a lot worse stuff than I was, and I think we were all holding our breath until we were on that freedom bird and in the air. I remember getting on the aircraft, the same one that brought our replacements in. We taxied out to the runway and turned and stopped. With that stop, everyone's hearts stopped to. We sure were a big target and we all knew what that meant. It was only 30 seconds, but it could have been a lifetime. No one moved or said a word, but as soon as we were airborne, what a great applause. I think it could have lasted until we landed in Japan, our first stop home. From Japan, we went to Alaska. It is always cold in Alaska. Well, from the Nam to Alaska it sure seemed it. I cleared customs in Alaska and then it was on to California and my freedom for the rest of my life. All I had to do was make it through, and I did. Nothing but gravy now. Thank you, Lord.

Photos

Plate 1 - Viet Cong Headquarters on second night of the Tet Offensive.

Plate 2 - Our way to get snipers. The field we set on fire.

Plate 3 - A large wrecker used to block the Main Gate during the first days of TET

Plate 4 - Our Jeep hit by RPG

Plate 5 - The car that tried to attack our house with a RPG and stopped by gunfire

Plate 6 -Another car hit by our artillery

Plate 7 - **Troops with an armored Jeep clearing** snipers

Plate 8 - Bartender at bar I went to on base.

Plate 9 -Author in front of small trucks used to haul sand

Plate 10 - Bullet went between driver and me with armored personnel carrier (APC) arriving for rescue

Plate 11 - Picture taken next day showing the knoll where bullet came from. Note shotgun rider on front truck on convoy duty

Plate 12 - Wagner sitting crater left by mortar round that landed behind him while on perimeter patrol

Plate 13 - 20 mm truck replacing wrecker
guarding Main Gate

Plate 14 - Later during TET a tank was moved up to guard the Main Gate. The buses are being used as a road block

Plate 15 - Truck that took concussion from rocket that saved my partner and me.

Plate 16 - Another angle of how the force blew the windshield out and peeled the hood up.

Plate 17 - First barracks in the Nam with no sandbags in site. Poor planning

Plate 18 - Barracks burning

Plate 19 - Barracks burning

Plate 20 - Building hit by rocket

Plate 21 - Caskets

Plate 22 - The Mule. The driver had a place to put his feet to run the gas pedal and clutch. Only one seat on the Mule.

Plate 23 - A photo of the driver's station on the Mule.

Plate 24 - My friend Toby pointing to the famous parachute on the Mule.

Plate 25 - The parachute attempt that didn't work

Plate 26 - Tan San Nhut Hospital

Plate 27 - Author on guard duty.

Plate 28 - Caribou cargo plane

Plate 29 - C-123 cargo plane

Plate 30 - Leaving Vietnam the hard way

Acknowledgements

I want to express appreciation to Amanda Foskett for the valuable job of editing my book into a readable form.

Credit to Morwenna Rakestraw for pulling a cover together that expresses in a concise manner the essence of my book.

Many thanks to Bill Martin for his guidance in completing this book.

Dear Reader,

Thank you for your selection of reading material. I hope this book measured up to your expectations. The most critical part for a new author is getting the word out to other readers.

I would appreciate your help in spreading the word. There are three important things you can do. If you do anything, go to Amazon.com and write a review.

1.   Go to Amazon.com and leave a review
2.   Tell a friend about this book
3.   Tell you your social network about this book.

Positive reviews made in various places will help readers find me.

Again, thanks for your support.

Larry Stoddard!

31434627R00157

Made in the USA
Columbia, SC
14 November 2018